the LONGEST ROAD

ROAD

Stories Along the Trans-Canada Highway

the LONGEST ROAD

ROAD

Stories
Along the
Trans-Canada
Highway

Red Deer PRESS

Bob Weber

The Publishers

Red Deer Press

813 MacKimmie Library Tower

2500 University Drive NW

Calgary, Alberta, Canada   T2N 1N4

www.reddeerpress.com

Credits

Cover and text design by Erin Woodward. Text designed along the Longest Road.

Cover photographs courtesy of Bruno Engler, Burt Brown, Randy Bachman, Peter Cotsworth, the Culver family and the Archives of Ontario

Back cover photograph courtesy John Marriot/JEM Photography

Printed and bound in Canada by Friesens for Red Deer Press

Acknowledgments

Financial support provided by the Canada Council, the Department of Canadian Heritage, the Alberta Foundation for the Arts, a beneficiary of the Lottery Fund of the Government of Alberta, and the University of Calgary.

THE CANADA COUNCIL | LE CONSEIL DES ARTS
FOR THE ARTS | DU CANADA
SINCE 1957 | DEPUIS 1957

Canadian Cataloguing in Publication Data

Weber, Bob, 1960–

The longest road : stories along the Trans-Canada Highway / Bob Weber.

ISBN 0-88995-279-5

1. Trans-Canada Highway. 2. Canada—Description and travel. I. Title.

FC75.W42 2003   971   C2003-905280-X

5 4 3 2 1

To my wife Sylvia, the navigator of all our road trips.

TRANS CANADA

CONTENTS

Prologue 9

Chapter 1 13

Chapter 2 21

Chapter 3 34

Chapter 4 50

Chapter 5 59

Chapter 6 71

Chapter 7 87

Epilogue 100

PROLOGUE

THE STORY OF THE CANADIAN ROAD BEGINS ON THE COUNTRY'S RIVERS.

In 1787 a fearless young fur trader arrived at a cabin on what was then the very fringe of civilization. Alexander Mackenzie had been assigned to the post on the Athabasca River in what is now northern Alberta by his employer, the North-West Company, as second-in-command to Peter Pond, a wily and occasionally violent veteran of the fur trade business. The pairing was serendipitous. Pond was nearing the end of an adventurous career, ready to pass on what he knew. Mackenzie, ambitious and bold, was ready to listen and burning to make his mark on the vast green unknown of the New World. Pond and Mackenzie were already heirs to two centuries of exploration. First the French explorers, then the transplanted Montreal-based Scots of the North-West Company, had opened a watery route all the way from the St. Lawrence River to the Saskatchewan to this remote cabin upstream from enormous Lake Athabasca. Much had been achieved by these birchbark buccaneers, but one crucial feat remained undone. No one had crossed the entire continent, stringing this immense new land together with a line from one end of the map to the other. So when Pond, 46, told the 24-year-old Mackenzie that he'd heard of a mighty river that would carry anyone brave enough to follow it all the way to the Pacific, the young trader knew he had found his mission. Crossing the continent became, wrote Mackenzie, "the favourite project of my own ambition."

In 1789 Mackenzie believed he'd found Pond's river. But the great watercourse that now bears his name took him north to the icy Beaufort Sea instead of west to the Pacific. A few years later, in May 1793, he tried again, following what is now the Peace River. That party—a clerk, six voyageurs, two Indians, and "a large, friendly dog," all in one 7-metre (25-foot) canoe—followed the Peace to the Rocky Mountains, scaled the Continental Divide and entered the watershed of the Fraser River. Eventually, they followed the Bella Coola River down to the Pacific. Mackenzie had become the first to cross North America, 13 years before the celebrated American explorers Lewis and Clark. He marked his bold deed with an understated matter-of-factness that today, more than two centuries later, seems uniquely Canadian. On a rock outcrop over a cove in Fitz Hugh Sound, with a combination of vermillion and bear grease, Mackenzie wrote: "Alex Mackenzie From Canada By Land 22d July 1793."

Mackenzie's was the crowning achievement of a Montreal-based fur trade empire that by the end of the 1700s had blazed a path up the St. Lawrence to the Mattawa and Ottawa rivers, over the height of land to Lake Nipissing, across Rainy Lake, the Lake of the Woods and Lake Winnipeg, up the North and South Saskatchewan rivers to the Rockies and down to the Pacific. It was almost 4,830 kilometres (3,000 miles) of hard travelling, and it took hard men. The voyageurs paddled 18 hours a day, 45 strokes to the minute. Routinely, they shouldered packs that weighed more than they did over long, rough, steep portages. They slept under their canoes and breakfasted, lunched and supped on greasy plate-fuls of pemmican—dried buffalo meat mashed with fat and berries. The voyageurs were vain, boastful, deceitful, violent and tough. They were also generous, fond of music, good times and women. They have been com-pared to members of a modern-day motorcycle gang, but their paddles brought the North-West under the commercial sway of the fledgling colony of Canada, making the future nation possible. In the words of for-mer Dominion Archivist W. Kaye Lamb, Mackenzie's canoe was "a needle drawing behind it a thread which . . . will form the basis of a network on which Canada still depends."

As Canada grew from colony to country, however, that network became less and less satisfactory. A tenuous trail of cart tracks, canoe routes and log forts may have sustained the fur trade, but it wouldn't suf-fice for the nation stretching from the Atlantic to the Pacific that John A. Macdonald, the first Prime Minister of the new Dominion of Canada, envisioned.

For his vision to become reality, Macdonald needed to bring the Pacific colony of British Columbia together with the rest of Confederation. But before B.C. would cast in its lot with Ontario, Quebec, Nova Scotia, New Brunswick, Prince Edward Island and Manitoba, it demanded some kind of link to the country it was to join. British Columbia's ultimatum was not the only pressing reason for the new nation to build a transportation link west. Whiskey traders and buffalo hunters were by this time well accus-tomed to following commercial routes from the northern plains down to Fort Benton, Montana, and then St. Paul, Minnesota, and everyone knew American expansionists were eager for the whole fertile territory to drop into their lap. So in 1871 Sir John promised British Columbia and the rest of his young nation an intercontinental railway. It would be the longest such line in the world, through some of Canada's most forbidding and thinly populated terrain—quite a task for a nation not yet five years old. Opposition politicians in the House of Commons called it "an act of insane recklessness." But it was built, the last spike driven on November 7, 1885. For the first time, immigrants could journey from Halifax to Vancouver, and western wheat could move from Regina to the Lakehead without detouring into the United States. The Canadian Pacific Railway has been called the national dream, and so it was. Like Mackenzie's canoe a century before, the first chugging locomotive of the CPR pulled the dream of a nation *a mari usque ad mare* along behind it.

Still, something was missing. On most frontiers, roads predated rail-ways. They were cheaper and faster to build, speeding the progress of settlers into the hinterland. A road system was cheaper to expand, too, especially since branch roads could be built to a lower standard. Roads were simply a faster way to fulfill the immigrants' dream of the New World: to move into the wilderness and conquer a piece of it to call their own. Sir Sanford Fleming, Canada's first chief engineer, understood that as early as 1862 when he advised that a system of roads should precede the rails. "The project of a highway to the Pacific is as old as the first settlement of Canada," he wrote that year in a report to the colonial legislature. His submission was accompanied by an extensive scouting report for such a road and a map of a possible route.

Fleming turned out to be right. Although rail became the first route across Canada, the construction of the CPR didn't diminish the need for roads. The railway could move wheat and immigrants by the carload, but it wasn't much use to the individual homesteader or prospector whose personal piece of the frontier lay beyond the rails. The settlers had travelled across continents and oceans to come to this new land, and they weren't content to let their dreams end where the tracks did. And so rough, primitive roads were built. One such road that even predated the Canadian Pacific Railway went from the Ontario Shield country to the prairies; by the 1890s, another led from the Pacific coast to the Cariboo gold fields. And as the century turned and the horse and buggy gave way to the transforming power of the automobile, good roads for personal transportation came to be understood more and more as part and parcel of personal freedom.

You can't hop on a train and just *go*. The railways are vehicles of mass transportation and agents of mass commerce. They make travel safe and predictable, but the movement of people and goods comes under the control of remote head offices, bound by schedules and priorities emanating from the centre, not the frontier. In the words of Canadian writer and philosopher John Ralston Saul, "This country's all about movement. It's all about communications—that's at the very heart of it. You really have to beware in a country like Canada of movement being defined by the elites." In a country where people strove to find their place in so much geography, something needed to open up Canada for Canadians.

In the early decades of the 20th century, in what was rapidly becoming the Age of the Automobile, a few intrepid drivers did try to drum up support for a coast-to-coast road through epic journeys, piloting their Reos and Model A's coast to coast, over pitted, muddy paths and corduroy trails constructed of logs. But before a growing and thinly populated country could build such a highway, there had to be a critical mass of young people on the move, a ready supply of vehicles to drive on it and the money to pay for it. Those conditions weren't met until after the Second World War, when a booming, confident and victorious Canada passed legislation that would create the Trans-Canada Highway. As Mackenzie and Macdonald had learned, however, Canada is a tough place for would-be continent-crossers. Shield, muskeg and mountains had to be traversed, and it would be yet another generation before the highway was complete.

When Europeans first landed on the shores of the New World, their immediate dream was to keep going, to see how far this new land stretched and to stretch themselves in reaching across it. This dream eventually turned into a country, and the dream is with us yet.

Millions of Canadians have lived that dream for themselves on the Trans-Canada Highway. What they found and what they learned about themselves and their country varies as widely as their reasons for hitting the asphalt in the first place. The mile-by-mile story of that road's construction, how it opened up the country, how it filled some communities and drained others, and how it freed desires is the people's history of the world's longest road.

CHAPTER 1

DENNIS CULVER WAS BORN IN 1923, RIGHT ABOUT THE SAME TIME AS THE AGE of the Automobile, and he grew up as one of its first children. His parents would always think of cars as something novel, but to Dennis they were simply a part of life. Every day there seemed to be more of them, huffing and backfiring along the previously quiet streets of Vancouver's Shaughnessy neighbourhood. Cars were shiny modern things that gleamed with possibility. Such objects have always held unending fascination for boys, and Dennis was no exception. Even before he was old enough for a license, he would sit in his father's Buick, backing it up and down the driveway of the family home, learning how the wonderful machine worked. And at a time before driving became a routine part of everyday life, family trips to the Rocky Mountains every summer steeped Dennis in the sense that car trips were romantic adventures.

The rattle and chug of the automobile was music to Dennis from the start, and people across the country were humming along with him. Canadians first fell hard for the automobile in the 1920s. Car ownership quadrupled to over a million during the decade, higher than any other countries except Great Britain and the United States. Road-building, fuelled by the then-enormous sum of $19 million committed by the government in far-off Ottawa, was happening everywhere in the young Dominion. In his fascination with cars, Dennis had plenty of company.

Dennis was so taken by things mechanical that his first choice in university was engineering, although he eventually switched to accounting. His studies, however, were about to be interrupted. Like so many other young men of his generation, he had to shift his plans into neutral as the Second World War cut in front of him. In 1942, at the age of 19, he signed up for the army. Naturally, he enlisted where he could be certain of encountering lots of interesting vehicles, and became an artillery officer with the Calgary Highlanders. A picture from the time shows him every inch the soldier: striding boldly ahead, kilt-clad, ramrod straight and luxuriantly mustachioed. To this day, he retains a hint of military bearing. His mustache, now snow-white, is still crisp.

Dennis was sent to Halifax for 18 months of training, learning to drive everything the army could put on wheels. Over the course of a year-and-a-half, however, a young man will find other things to occupy his time than military matters. On New Year's Eve in 1943, he was playing cribbage in the officer's mess when a striking young woman with the local branch of the Canadian Red Cross asked him to dance. Dennis put down his cards, and within a couple days was smitten enough to give her his artillery insignia badge and meet her family. The budding romance wasn't, however, to get any further. Duty intervened when the Red Cross moved his new girlfriend overseas and Dennis lost touch with her. Eventually, Dennis, too, was posted overseas, although as an infantry lieutenant, not as an artillery officer. "[The Nazis] weren't killing artillery officers fast enough," he recalls, "But they were still killing infantry officers, so off I went."

With the Highlanders, Dennis joined in the liberation of Holland, fighting sorties back and forth into Germany, crossing the Rhine and pushing one more time into Germany as the war ended. Because he had been a relative latecomer to the fighting, the army felt there were plenty of other soldiers who deserved to be sent home first, so Dennis was transferred to the Canadian Scottish regiment and stationed in Holland at war's end. He was to spend most of the next year keeping things orderly in his sector and making sure the members of his antitank platoon didn't get into too much trouble.

One day, Dennis' roommate, Monty, walked into their room and announced: "Culver, you and I are getting bushed. I've made us both a date for tomorrow night. We need some female companionship." Monty had lined up a nurse for himself and a Red Cross girl named Eleanor Wallace for Dennis. Dennis wasn't that keen at first, but after he met his date—a slim brunette with a confident, self-possessed air about her—his attitude quickly changed.

"At the end of the evening," says Dennis, "I turned to the Red Cross girl and I said, 'How about tomorrow night?' And it was tomorrow night and tomorrow night every single night." After about a month, Dennis and Eleanor were having dinner when an acquaintance of Eleanor's walked up and addressed her by a nickname that seemed oddly familiar. Suddenly, Dennis realized that the girl he was falling for was the same one to whom he'd given his artillery badge back in Halifax. To this day he can't explain why he didn't recognize her immediately. Maybe it was her different uniform. Maybe it was the passage of time. Maybe it was the sheer improbability of meeting the same girl again on a blind date half a world away. "I have asked Eleanor many times whether she recognized me, but I have never received a definitive answer," Dennis chuckles. Perhaps it's better to believe that Dennis and Eleanor fell in love at first sight—twice.

The couple spent as much of the next few months together as they could, driving through Europe in army jeeps, dining in officer's clubs, staying in hotels reserved for soldiers. More than once, Monty was awakened in the early hours by Dennis returning from Eleanor's hospital, about 50 kilometres (30 miles) away.

Finally, the idyll ended. Both Dennis and Eleanor were returned to Canada—she to Halifax, he to Vancouver. They could hardly have been farther apart, and in a time when only the rich travelled by airplane and a long-distance telephone call was an event, that was a serious problem. Dennis and Eleanor wrote occasional letters, but the romance began to sputter as both turned their attention to building civilian lives. Eleanor

Dennis and Eleanor enjoyed a brief idyll together in Europe after World War II, but were soon to find themselves separated by the width of a continent when they were returned home by their respective branches of service.[1]

found work as a secretary, and Dennis returned to the accountancy training he had started before the war.

Dennis, however, did stay in touch with his wartime buddy, Monty, whose life was moving forward more quickly. Like so many other returned soldiers, Monty had married and was expecting a baby. One day in August 1948 Dennis was helping Monty fix up a new apartment for his growing family. Maybe the nest-feathering got Dennis thinking, for he turned to Monty and said, "You know, I miss that Wallace woman." Despite Dennis' seeming nonchalance about his wartime romance, Monty had some idea of how deeply "that Wallace woman" had affected his friend. "Call her up," Monty advised. So Dennis did, catching up with Eleanor in Montreal.

Eleanor agreed to meet him there and come back with him to Vancouver for a visit. Her sister Joan would come along as a chaperone. Dennis had always loved driving, but on this trip he outdid himself, motoring all the way from Vancouver to Montreal in three days—heading, of course, through the United States, for Canada still had no national highway network. He brought the women back to the coast, where they quickly found jobs in the booming post-war economy. The couple had no trouble picking up where they had left off in Holland, and Eleanor became a spring bride in April 1950.

Spring seemed to be more than a season that year. The out-of-work, out-of-hope nation that had joined the fighting in 1939 found itself prosperous and confident at the war's victorious conclusion. Canada's economy had doubled in size between 1939 and 1945 and wasn't showing signs of stopping. The government instituted generous education and business grants for returning soldiers, and fears that there would be no jobs for them to return to proved groundless. A country that had played a big role in beating the Nazis and whose voice was heard on the world stage was now turning its attention to tackling big tasks at home. Transportation and communication, those old Canadian preoccupations, were prominent among them. The Trans-Canada Highway Act was passed in 1949. That same year, Newfoundland joined Confederation, completing the country's stretch across the continent. The Canadian Broadcasting Corporation, already a national radio voice, added its television service in 1952. In the early 1950s, debate began on a pipeline to carry Alberta's natural gas to the industrial heartland of Ontario. In 1954 Canada signed an agreement with the United States to build the St. Lawrence Seaway. Two years later, the Canso Causeway linked Cape Breton Island to the mainland for the first time.

Service stations, complete with smartly turned-out attendants, were only one of the many ways that the automobile changed the look of cities in Canada.[2]

It seemed that everywhere in the country everything was on the move, from natural resources to great ships to new forms of communication to everyday people in their everyday lives. Everything encouraged it. Families were growing. Jobs were plentiful. Unemployment, less than two percent in 1951, remained low almost the entire decade. The jobs paid better and better, too. For every dollar the average Canadian earned in 1951, there was $1.50 by the end of the decade. New federal government programs made it easier than ever for average Canadians to own homes. In vast numbers, the move to the suburbs began. During the first five years after the war, nearly 350,000 new homes were constructed, nearly all of them in new suburban subdivisions sprouting from former farmlands and forests on the outskirts of cities.

The suburbs accelerated the growth of the culture of movement as if pressing the pedal to the floor. People in the old urban neighbourhoods shopped and worked close to their homes, but dwellers in the new developments had to get in and out of them every day. Suburban moms needed to shop and suburban dads needed to get to work. Commuting became a way of life. By 1958 one report stated the average Toronto worker spent nearly an hour a day getting to his job. And most of that traffic was by car, as rail passenger traffic began to decline for the first time in Canadian history. Provinces were building roads as fast as they could afford them, but they still couldn't keep up. In 1951 there were nearly 17 registered vehicles for every surfaced mile of road. A mere five years later, that figure had risen to more than 20.

The Age of the Automobile that began when Dennis was a boy was now becoming a full-blown car culture. The look of Canadian cities was permanently changed as gasoline alleys began to ring their outskirts, expressways cut through them and service stations sprouted on their busiest corners.

Old businesses adapted to the new priorities. Drive-in restaurants fed the new urban nomads. Motels, where you could drive your car right up to your room and park it there overnight, housed them when they travelled. Drive-in theatres, where mom and dad could watch the show while kids slept in the roomy backseats of Bel Airs and Fairlanes, entertained them.

Shopping changed, too. Canada's first shopping centre was built in Montreal in 1949; the second opened the following year in West Vancouver. National franchises began to spread, capitalizing on the traveller's desire to find a familiar recognizable name.

Motor hotels, or motels, sprouted up all along the Trans-Canada. This 1961 picture from Swift Current, Saskatchewan, shows some were open even before the highway was finished.[4]

One of the ways the new emphasis on mobility and convenience was expressed was through the proliferation of drive-in restaurants, where the waitresses became car-hops and you didn't even have to leave the comfort of your big bench seat behind the wheel to grab a bite.[3]

Everything worked together. After 15 years of hard times and war, Canadians believed in the future again. And the symbol of their new faith became the car, the rubber-and-steel manifestation of the new realities of movement, money and modernity. The vehicles themselves reflected the times, their tailfins and exaggerated chrome ornamentation inspired by

Not only could you now eat in your car, you could be entertained there, too. This drive-in theatre screen going up in Saskatoon, Saskatchewan, in 1953 was only one of hundreds that were erected across Canada.[5]

These 1953 Fords rolling off the assembly line in Windsor, Ontario, were among the thousands of new vehicles of all kinds being eagerly snapped up by Canadians from coast to coast.[6]

rocket ships and jet airplanes, the very icons of the new age. Just over half of Canadian households had a car at the start of the 1950s. By the end of the decade, that figure had grown to nearly 70 percent. In absolute numbers, car registrations nearly doubled from 3.6 million to more than six million between 1954 and 1963.

Optimistic, flush with cash and eager to get on with their lives, Canadians set to the business of building homes, establishing careers and raising families like never before. North America's great baby boom had began, and nowhere was it echoing louder than in Canada. Between 1949 and 1959 Canada's population grew almost 30 percent to 17.5 million—one of the highest birth rates in the world and still the largest single-decade percentage increase in the country's history.

Dennis and Eleanor did their part. Within ten years, they had nine children: Noni (1951), Dan (1953), Margot (1953), Bruce (1955), the twins Diana and Sheila (1956), Hugh (1958), Susan (1959) and Ronald (1961). In a busy, growing country, few households were busier or grew faster.

Although Dennis had chosen accounting over engineering, he retained his love of things mechanical. He began the 1950s as the chief financial officer for an engine factory, largely so he could be near some revolving gears. Eventually, however, he struck out and opened his own accounting firm. He got his machinery fix through regular travel. When the firm opened a branch in Tofino on the west side of Vancouver Island, the Culvers got used to regular road trips out to the wild Pacific shore.

Proudly posed in front of their Mercedes touring bus, the entire Culver family was now ready to take to the road in comfort and safety after years of tight quarters.[7]

The Longest Road

Over the decade, room in the car got to be to be more and more of a problem. Although the Culvers would have filled any one of the tail-finned, two-toned monsters that were coming out of Detroit, things were even tighter in Dennis' Rover 75, a rather stately British car built to accommodate two in the front and three in the back. By 1961 his family filled it to bursting. On trips, Dennis drove and Eleanor took the front passenger seat. She held the baby, and another child sat between mom and dad on a cushion atop the transmission tunnel. The two oldest children sat in folding wooden seats at either side of the rear bench seat, while the remaining five kids squeezed into the back seat, breathing in sequence and hoping no one developed an itch. It never was a satisfactory way to get around (it would have horrified modern safety advocates), and it wasn't getting any roomier as the kids grew.

Dennis eventually discovered the ideal vehicle for his family. He saw it in a Mercedes-Benz dealership one day in 1960 on his way home from work—an 11-seat touring bus, complete with reclining seats and panoramic passenger windows that curved into the roof. It was perfect. It cost, however, $10,000—enough money in those days to buy a modest house. Dennis had told the salesman to give him a call if the price ever came down, but he knew it would have to fall a long way before it was within the reach of a chartered accountant just starting out on his own. About two years later, though, the salesman did call. The resort that had originally purchased the bus had decided to sell it off. The Culvers stuffed into the Rover to drive over for a look at it, and the kids marveled at the luxury of having their own seats. With a little haggling, Dennis got the price down to $3,000. He drove the bus home a few days later. He planned to surprise everyone by turning off the engine and coasting into the driveway.

The rattling, chugging Mercedes diesel, however, was audible three blocks away, especially as it ground up the hill to the Culver's neighbourhood. Instead of a surprise, there were nine little kids, jumping up and down and shouting with excitement. The Culvers were finally ready to join in the spirit of the times. Advertising, movies and songs had mythologized V-8 powered, rocket-finned cars as freedom machines; now, although it was a blocky, diesel-powered, gray-and-white bus, the Culvers finally had a four-wheeled liberator of their own.

New machines create new possibilities, and within weeks the bus gave Dennis an inspiration. Eleanor came from a large, close, east coast family. In fact, at their wedding Dennis had been slightly shocked to discover that he had not only acquired a wife, but 64 new nieces and nephews. The extensive Wallace clan had never met any of the fine, thriving brood their transplanted west coast daughter was raising. Stranded on the other side of the continent, Eleanor missed her family and longed to connect them with her children. But there was simply no affordable way for a young businessman to fly the whole family across the country. Dennis decided to pile the whole family in their new bus and drive to Halifax for Eleanor's mother's birthday on June 27. Just months before, Prime Minister John Diefenbaker had presided over the official opening of a new route—paved, graded and safe—clear across the country. The Trans-Canada Highway was brand new; the Culvers had new wheels just itching for some asphalt. It was time for a road trip.

CHAPTER 2

The Culvers' timing was perfect. Even a year earlier, the Halifax trip that Dennis and Eleanor began planning that spring would not have been possible. Until the summer of 1962, there was no single, modern, upgraded route to take Canadians from one end of their country to the other. Even then, some stretches still weren't finished, especially in Newfoundland. But when Dennis coasted the Mercedes into his driveway that December, it had only been a few months since the official opening of the Trans-Canada Highway.

There had been roads before the Trans-Canada, of course. Dennis recalls camping trips with his parents in the interior of B.C. back in the 1930s and '40s. Asphalt stretched as far as Chilliwack, then it was gravel the rest of the way—a narrow, twisting way that clung to mountainsides far above the raging Kicking Horse River. Nobody's car jack got rusty, for blowouts were inevitable. On one family trip, Dennis watched his father fix 11 flats. And bad roads weren't confined to the mountains. When Dennis brought Eleanor back from Montreal in 1948, the party got just west of

Sudbury when a rock knocked the bottom out of the car's battery, dumping acid all over the engine compartment. That same trip, flying gravel punctured the gas tank as they went through Jasper National Park. Dennis soldered in a nail to plug the hole, praying the remaining gas in the tank didn't explode.

Before the Trans-Canada, roads were not only occasionally hazardous, but were also sometimes so roundabout as to be almost useless. British Columbia's old Big Bend Highway was hailed as a major breakthrough when it opened in 1940 after 11 years of work. But it wound and twisted through 305 kilometres (190 miles) of gravel to connect Revelstoke and Golden, communities only 92 kilometres (57 miles) apart. And in the winter, even that circuitous connection was closed. There was an even worse example in the Canadian Shield country of northern Ontario. The towns of Geraldton and Hearst were about 240 kilometres (150 miles) apart. But the shortest drive between the two was 3,330 kilometres (2,070 miles) long, all the way around the Great Lakes and through the United States.

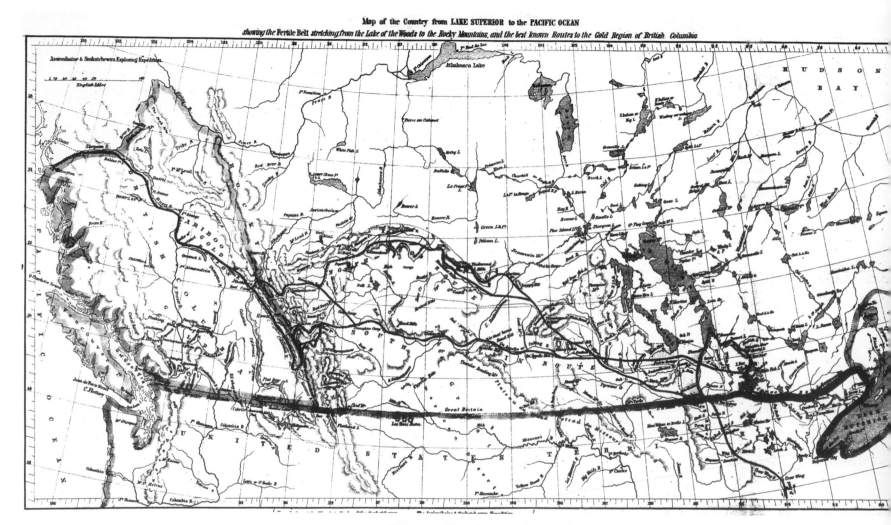

Map of the Country from LAKE SUPERIOR to the PACIFIC OCEAN
showing the Fertile Belt stretching from the Lake of the Woods to the Rocky Mountains, and the best known Routes to the Gold Region of British Columbia

After a long scouting trip, Henry Youle Hind drew up this map showing proposed routes for a network of cross-Canada highways. Although John A. Macdonald's governing Conservatives decided a railway should precede the road, roads were eventually built along most of Hind's planned pathways.[8]

A fast, safe, modern highway that would allow trips like the one the Culvers planned had been a long time coming. Five years before Confederation, Sir Sanford Fleming, Canada's legendary chief engineer, laid out the need in a report to the colonial legislature. In fact, Fleming, who became a tireless builder of roads and railways throughout the young Dominion, believed the young, soon-to-be nation should focus on building a road across its width instead of a railway. Canada just didn't have the resources yet for a transcontinental railway, he believed; nor would it have enough population along its route to make it economic for years to come. A highway route chosen with foresight and planning would build customers for the railway by encouraging settlement. The railway could be twinned with the road when circumstances were favourable. Little daunted by trackless prairie and the jagged ramparts of the Rockies, Fleming proposed an orderly, three-tiered system of roads, beginning with a main trunk line on 45 metres (150 feet) of allowance with shelterbelts of trees along its length to keep down the snowdrifts and provide fuel and repair stock for the eventual railway. Fleming's conclusions were supported by the account of the geographer Henry Youle Hind, who submitted an extensive scouting report of possible routes as part of the same document. Hind included a map, which more or less followed the paths established by generations of canoes and Red River carts. His map indicated that the Rockies should be scaled to the north, through the Yellowhead Pass.

But Fleming knew that his surveyors would turn up something better in the south, closer to the fertile belt. Such a pass "has been or may be discovered across the Rocky Mountains," he wrote—the blithe, characteristic faith of his age in the ability of science and engineering to subdue thousands of kilometres of wilderness.

Fleming had it all figured out. It couldn't take more than four years to survey the line across Canada to the mouth of the Fraser, he wrote. Another two years would suffice to put in a dirt road across its entire length. And within 17 years, the entire road could be brought up to the very best of modern standards from Lake Superior to the burgeoning port of Vancouver. And the whole vast work could be completed for the "comparatively trifling annual outlay" of one dollar per capita, assuming a gradual population increase. Fleming wrote:

> "It must be obvious that the progress of the new territories, as well as their future and permanent social and commercial wants, would be much influenced by a pre-arrangement of the various lines of internal communication, and it must be equally clear that to attain the highest degree of easy intercourse between every section at the least outlay of capital and labour every road of whatever class should be considered as a portion of a whole system."

To which one can only add, QED.

Fleming wasn't alone in assuming a road would be the first link across the new Dominion. James Douglas, the governor of British Columbia, would have initially been happy to settle for a road as he negotiated to bring his province into Confederation. But somebody told him to hold out for a railway, and a railway it was to be. Nevertheless, roads were eventually built along most of the route that Hind proposed.

In British Columbia, the Cariboo Gold Rush of the 1860s was the spur for Douglas to order the construction of what came to be known as the Cariboo Road. It offered 620 kilometres (385 miles) of graded wagon road

The Longest Road

from Yale, where the Fraser becomes too wild for navigation, to the gold-laden creeks and raucous saloons of Barkerville. In places, the road ran near enough the Fraser to catch the spray from its rapids; elsewhere it was so far above the river that a rock thrown from its edge would disappear from sight before it hit the water. Sometimes its path had to be blasted through the mountainside; sometimes it clung to great piles of wooden trestles. When it opened in 1864, it allowed wagon trains to pass where only mules had gone before.

Seen here at the height of the Cariboo Gold Rush, Barkerville was one of the rough-and-ready prospector's towns along the Cariboo Road. The Trans-Canada was eventually to closely follow its path.[9]

In the east, the Dawson Road, named after the engineer who designed it, ran from the Lake of the Woods to the Red River country and was partly built by Canadian soldiers heading west to put down the 1870 Red River Rebellion. They carried construction supplies and military equipment over 47 portages, some over a mile long and some around waterfalls so high that the men had to haul their York boats up steep ladders. The 225 kilometres (140 miles) of corduroy road they built, coupled with 565 kilometres (350 miles) of boat travel, became a vital link for construction crews building the railway that eventually supplanted it.

By the mid-1870s, roads ran from the Pacific shore east to the western wall of the Coast Mountains. From the east, wagons could move from the Lakehead to the Red River Valley, and from there follow well-established cart tracks such as the Carlton Trail west to the eastern slopes of the Rockies. The road system had grown up very nearly along the lines that Hind had said it should. Two main gaps remained: the Canadian Shield over the Great Lakes, and the mountains of British Columbia and Alberta.

For decades, that's how it remained as railways, not roads, preoccupied the national imagination. Locomotives were to the Victorians what computer networks are to their 21st century successors: the ultimate tool and emblem of their society. All talk of a Trans-Canada road ceased for generations while tracks were built for the iron horse.

But the idea of a road across the country never entirely went away. Finally, in 1910, a group of western motorists founded the Canadian Highway Association to promote good roads. At the group's second convention in Victoria, British Columbia, in 1912, it struck a gold medal to be given to the first driver to travel overland by car all the way across Canada.

This optimistic group of road boosters in Port Alberni, British Columbia, were gathered in 1912 for the planting of what they hoped would become the first signpost of the Trans-Canada Highway. The fulfillment of their dream, however, would take another 50 years.[10]

This was no small challenge. At the time, roads were in such a state that making the 140-kilometre (82-mile) trip from St. Stephen to St. John, New Brunswick, in 12 hours was considered good time. A popular bit of doggerel summed up the roads in southern Ontario:

> . . . But from somewhere east of Suez
> Where the roads are at their worst,
> Down to rocky Alabama
> Of the motorists accursed,
> For bumps and thrills and all the ills

Canadian roads in the early days of driving weren't only muddy and pitted. Sometimes they were little more than glorified mule or cart tracks, as this precipitous cliffside trail demonstrates.[11]

> That, travelling, one gets onto
> The greatest jar you give your car
> Is Hamilton to Toronto.

The Longest Road

Nevertheless, a worthy dare will always find a taker, and the first would-be four-wheeled Mackenzie was an Englishman named Thomas Wilby, who thought it would be a good lark to drive his big Reo tourer from Halifax to Victoria.

Englishman Thomas Wilby (left) and his Canadian mechanic Jake Haney, seen here by the back of their Reo tourer, were the first to attempt to drive across Canada.[12]

Wilby and his Canadian mechanic, F.V. (Jake) Haney, dipped their vehicle's rear wheels in the Atlantic on August 27, 1914. Fifty-two days later, they actually made it, and Wilby dumped a flask of Halifax harbor water into the Pacific.

The route had been anything but easy. At one point, the two-tonne vehicle was almost completely swallowed by Ontario muskeg; at another, steep inclines snapped its drive train; at other times, it sunk up to its hubs in gumbo. Wilby and Haney had teetered along precipitous mountain trails, dodged boulders in the Shield and gotten completely lost on the prairies. Once, Wilby and Haney were forced to drive on railway tracks at night through the mountains.

Rickety stream crossings such as this were often the least of Wilby and Haney's problems. Many times, the real trouble began when they got off the bridge and onto the muddy, pitted road.[13]

Because their Reo, in various states of disrepair, had on occasion been hauled by horses, trains and boats, they were ineligible to receive the Canadian Highway Association's medal. Nevertheless, their adventure inspired Canadians from coast to coast. Every time they pulled into a town, cheering crowds lined the streets and business boosters talked up road-building. But still, no highway.

Across the sandy beach and into the Pacific—Wilby and Haney made it across the country, but because they hadn't made it entirely under their own steam, their sometimes literally trail-blazing adventure didn't win them the gold medal.[14]

The Longest Road

The highway lobbying increased during the 1920s. People like A.W. Campbell, the federal government's chief commissioner of highways, kept up the pressure.

This 1923 scene was all too familiar for drivers of the day: a truck up to its axles in muck and sweating, grunting men trying to lever and dig it out. Situations like this were the reason men like Perry Doolittle worked so hard to get roads and highways improved.[15]

But it was Dr. Perry Doolittle, the legendary head of the Canadian Automobile Association, who was undoubtedly the best-known public face behind the movement for good roads. Ever dapper and immaculately groomed no matter what automotive horror he'd just experienced, Doolittle drove back and forth across the country at least three times to rev up enthusiasm for road-building. Then in his 60s, Doolittle may have been the most imperturbable motorist to have ever rolled rubber in Canada. Dodging falling rocks while driving through the mountains was

nothing to him; nor was having to get out of the vehicle and roll the big ones off the road. A foot of snow was but a spot of bother, and narrow, shoulderless roads that clung to cliffsides were all part of the fun. When mud packed his vehicle from wheel rim to floorbed, he hired a horse and towed the car into town. And everywhere he stopped, the good doctor would buttonhole the nearest reporter and deliver yet another encomium on the importance of good roads.

In 1919 the Canadian government came up with $20 million to improve the nation's network of roads, which had resulted in a sort of piece-by-piece, province-by-province route across the country—with the exception of Lake Superior's northern shore. In 1925, Ed Flickenger, a curious photographer employed by the Ford Motor Company, decided to see what this new route was like and hit the road in a brand-new Model T, accompanied by none other than the unflappable Dr. Doolittle. The two found 6,440 kilometres (4,000 miles) of reasonable highway, although it varied from concrete and asphalt to plain old dirt. But they still had to install flanged steel wheels on the car and drive on railway tracks for 1,370 kilometres (850 miles), so they, too, were ruled ineligible for the Canadian Highway Association's gold medal. The association itself had long since disbanded in the face of the seeming hopelessness of their goal.

In the 1930s, Ottawa finally responded with another $20 million, perhaps grasping that road-building was a good way to put people to work during the Depression. That road-building created just the opportunity a young man named Burt Brown had been waiting for.

Today, Burt is a dapper, silver-haired, straight-backed 97-year-old who still looks completely at home in the Shield country he helped open up. Back then, he was a young man convinced that the automobile was the wave

Burt Brown spent a lifetime around cars—first building them, then refuelling them and creating a destination for their city-weary drivers in the pristine Shield country of northern Ontario.[16]

of the future. For a while, he was an employee of Toronto's Durant auto factory, and when he wasn't building cars, he was learning about them.

But when the Depression closed the Durant plant in 1933, Burt was left temporarily without prospects. Then he got a tip from an in-law who was a surveyor for the provincial government: a new road that would eventually become Highway 17 was going to be built into the Shield. It would run by a nice little spot along the English River, just beside a small lake about midway between Kenora and Thunder Bay. One day, that site would see a lot of traffic. Burt had been thinking about getting into the gasoline business, and this sounded like an ideal opportunity. He decided to take a look at the area, which was still so raw that he had to cross-country ski from

the nearest train stop. He liked what he saw and cut a deal with Imperial Oil to supply gas and put in pumps. He skidded some old bunkhouses over a rough construction road and was ready for business even before the highway was.

There were two highway camps within a few kilometres of his service station, Burt remembers, mostly full of school teachers and city workers who couldn't find other jobs during the Depression. The government paid them five dollars a month plus room and board. It was last-resort work for people with few options, little experience and less skill. Nevertheless, Burt watched them punch a road through the bush despite the primitive conditions and the low pay. It was quite an achievement, and for a while the road construction generated considerable excitement. Opening day—July 1, 1935—saw a cavalcade of cars drive down the gravel surface. But after that, the country was nearly as deserted as before.

Burt Brown's gas station near the English River along what would become Ontario's Highway 17 was an oasis on a lonely, treacherous length of road for 1930s-era travellers.[17]

"I always maintained that 50 percent of the cars would stop," Burt says. "And on some days, they *both* did."

Still, Burt says there was always somebody on the move in those days, always somebody trying to find a place where there was work, family to lean on or simply hope. Money was tight for those Depression-era travellers. Once, a woman offered Burt her diamond ring in payment for a tank of gas. He gave her the fuel, slipped her a little cash to keep her going and kept that ring for her until she sent him the gas money.

And the road itself was still a rough passage. In the summer, mud could make it impassable, stranding campers and travellers in the middle of nowhere.

Burt saw a lot of this in his early days at English River—frustrated campers spending their precious holiday time having their vehicle towed instead of enjoying the fishing and swimming.[18]

In the winter, snow could shut things down just as quickly. The road hadn't changed the area much, and Burt might as well have still been living in the bush. With his nearest neighbour, an Indian hunting and fishing guide, living a quarter of a mile away, Burt spent his first winter at the station completely on his own. Month after month, he did odd jobs, chopped wood to stay warm and listened to the radio for company in his little cabin near the pumps. It was so still that when the snowplow from Thunder Bay pushed through, he could hear it for two days before it actually arrived.

By the end of the Depression, however, Burt's lonely stretch of the Shield was becoming an anomaly. Ontario and Quebec had an increasingly well-developed and modern highway system, the roads through the prairies were mostly dependable and even the mountains of B.C. and Alberta had passable if indirect routes. There remained, however, big gaps in the Canadian Shield. On the north shore of Lake Superior, about 195 kilometres (120 miles) of trackless forest, rock and muskeg stretched from roughly about the community of Marathon to Agawa Bay west of Sault Ste. Marie. And farther north, there was still that 240-kilometre (150-mile) gap between Hearst and Geraldton—although a rough but serviceable road that became Highway 11 was opened in 1946. Within months, Brig. R.A. MacFarlane took advantage of it and drove a new Chevy from Louisbourg, Nova Scotia, to Victoria, British Columbia, in nine days to complete the first real coast-to-coast car trip and claim the old Canadian Highway Association's gold medal—34 years after it was first offered.

The dream of building a Canadian national road link entered the home stretch on December 10, 1949, when "An Act to encourage the construction of a Trans-Canada Highway" became law.

Even after the Trans-Canada Highway Act was signed in 1949, bureaucrats and politicians met for months to hammer out the details of the great project's construction. This 1950 photo shows one such meeting in a committee room on Parliament Hill.[19]

The Liberal government of Mackenzie King calculated that it would take about seven years to close the Shield gap and upgrade the rest of the road. The road was to be paved with asphalt and would measure at least 6.5 metres (22 feet) wide with no more than a six percent grade. Sight lines had to be such that a driver could see an object 15 centimetres (six inches) high at 180 metres (600 feet). Bridge clearances had to be at least 4.5 metres (14.5 feet). Because the highway would have to compete with American routes for truck traffic, it was to be built wherever possible within about 320 kilometres (200 miles) of the border. This being Canada, there was a carefully defined division of financing between the federal and provincial governments. Ottawa would pay half, up to $150 million.

Of course, nothing worked out as planned. The final work wasn't complete until 1970. This being Canada, the provinces also went back to Ottawa to plead for more money, eventually persuading the central government to agree to also assume 90 percent of the cost of the toughest, most expensive ten percent of the road in each province. The federal government wound up paying closer to $900 million, with the provinces contributing another $600 million.

Many sections of the route had been cobbled together from previously existing and upgraded provincial highways, which is why the Trans-Canada has different numbers in different parts of the country. But at long last, Canada finally had its ocean-to-ocean road link: 7,700 kilometres (4,784 miles) from rugged Atlantic coast through the busy factory cities of southern Ontario, across the forbidding Shield, past the green and rolling prairies, over the castellated peaks of the Rockies down to the rain forests of the Pacific shores. It was, and remains, the longest *national* highway in the world.

The official opening ceremonies were held September 3, 1962—100 years after Fleming filed his historic report. Fleming would have smiled at the chosen site, too. Prime Minister John Diefenbaker and various provincial highways ministers gathered at the summit of the Rogers Pass, the pass that was found just where Fleming had assumed it eventually would be.

True, the highway wasn't exactly finished. Upgrading and construction would go on for almost another decade. But it was passable from coast to coast, and the speeches were fulsome in their praise—indeed, the ceremony took three hours, with remarks from a generous selection of provincial

About 2,000 people gathered for the opening ceremonies of the Trans-Canada Highway high atop the Rogers Pass—not far from where the opening of that other great Canadian transportation route, the Canadian Pacific Railway, was celebrated.[20]

politicians and highway promoters, as well as moments of unintentional comedy. Saskatchewan's highways minister C.G. Willis told the crowd of about 2,000 how pleased he was to be in the province of Quebec. His B.C. counterpart, "Flying Phil" Gagliardi, delivered his *personal* thanks to the Almighty for arranging the beautiful weather. And while the band of the

Princess Patricia's Canadian Light Infantry was on hand, the musicians had to be content with looking splendid in their dress uniforms. Their instruments had somehow gone astray in transit, and music was provided by a lone piper.

Meanwhile, back in Newfoundland, Premier Joey Smallwood was fuming. While the rest of Canada celebrated their smooth new road, the Trans-Canada was only half-finished on The Rock and, like a TV show, was coming slightly later in Newfoundland. "Deceit, humbug and bluff," huffed Smallwood.

Still, the official opening of the Trans-Canada Highway was a moment of genuine achievement, being marked about 150 kilometres (90 miles) from Craigellachie, where the last spike of the Canadian Pacific Railway had been driven.

Prime Minister John Diefenbaker knew a moment of national import and symbolism when he saw one. And although the crowd missed most of his speech when he grabbed the microphone of a nearby radio reporter instead of the public address system, Dief closed out the ceremony in fine rhetorical form:

> "This ceremony today marks another step in the completion of the dreams of the Fathers of Confederation, dreams of a united and growing nation moving forward in faith that Canada's destiny is that of an ever greater and always independent nation. May this highway, the longest high-standard highway in all the world, bring Canadians together, bring a renewed determination to all Canadians to do their part to make this nation worthy of its destiny."

Opening the Trans-Canada Highway was a triumphant day for Prime Minister John Diefenbaker. The ardent nationalist was completing the dream that began during the time of his political hero, John A. Macdonald.[21]

CHAPTER 3

Diefenbaker's ringing phrase about the new highway "bringing Canadians together" would have brought appreciative nods from Dennis and Eleanor—if either of them had had time to think about it. Taking two adults and nine children aged one to eleven on a 6,440-kilometre (4,000-mile) road trip in an unfamiliar vehicle took a serious amount of planning and preparation. Ever the accountant, Dennis totaled up his assets and liabilities.

Time, for example, would be a definite liability. June was a busy time for Dennis at the office, and he knew he couldn't afford to be away from it for much more than a week. So if he flew back from Halifax by himself, that meant he had about five days for the drive. And although the Mercedes was the asset that made the whole project possible, it carried some liabilities, too. Namely, it weighed 1,815 kilograms (4,000 pounds) unloaded and was powered by a 45 horsepower engine. In other words, it was solid and roomy, but slow. Just how slow became evident one weekend when the whole family hopped in and took a 2,415-kilometre (1,500-mile)

shakedown cruise. Top average speed turned out to be about 65 kilometres (40 miles) per hour. Dennis did a little math. The distance to Halifax would be 5,470 kilometres (3,400 miles), give or take. To cover that distance in five days meant they would have to log about 1,095 kilometres (680 miles) per day. At 65 kilometres an hour, the bottom line was 17 out of every 24 hours had to be spent on the road.

Clearly, if a family the size and age of Dennis and Eleanor's was going to drive 17 hours a day for five days, they couldn't just hit the pavement and hope that hotels, service stations, restaurants and bathrooms would materialize along the road whenever they were required. The Culvers needed a plan. For four months, Dennis went to bed every night with a road map and a calendar. On the map, he plotted every village, hamlet, campground and picnic shelter he could find, calculating the distance and driving time between them. Then he took his calendar and broke down the entire odyssey into five 1,095 kilometre (680-mile) legs. Cross-referencing between the map and the calendar, Dennis worked it out so that every morning at 8:00 A.M. the bus would arrive at a public campground or picnic site for a three-hour break. Eleanor would fix breakfast while everyone stretched their legs, got a little fresh air and used the toilets. Dennis would quickly check the vehicle over, then grab a two-hour nap. Eleanor and the kids would unpack, cook, clean and restow the kitchen. At precisely 11:00 A.M., Dennis would hop in the driver's seat and away they'd go. Six hours later, the whole process would repeat itself for supper.

It was also clear that if 11 people were going to spend 17 hours a day inside that bus, it was going to need a little modification. A roof rack was installed. Dennis put the backseat armrests on hinges so they could be flipped up to make a comfortable bed for whichever adult wasn't driving. Eleanor sewed curtains to hang up around the windows and to separate the front two seats from the rest of the bus. An auxiliary fuel tank was installed so the bus could travel 1,125 kilometres (700 miles) without refueling. A sliding table in front of the front passenger seat allowed the co-pilot to assemble sandwiches on the road; another, larger table could be hooked onto the outside of the vehicle during rest periods. Extra batteries were installed to power lights and devices such as Dennis' electric razor. Dennis even wove a hammock that could be suspended from the side pillars where baby Ron could sleep.

Finally, some accommodation had to be made for bathroom breaks. Mom and dad had done enough travelling with the kids to know that pit stops six hours apart weren't going to be enough. But if they stopped every time someone called out from the back, they'd never be able to keep their schedule. It could easily take most of an hour to cycle nine kids and two adults through a roadside privy. Besides, Dennis knew it took a few kilometres and another ten minutes just to get the bus back up to speed,

especially when fully loaded. Repeat that exercise a few times a day and their five days would be up before they even got out of the prairies. So Dennis and Eleanor came up with the only solution they could: a bottle for the boys and a honey bucket for the girls, both stashed in the stairwells by the side doors. The boys didn't mind. In fact, they took a manly pride in how quickly and how often they could fill up the bottle. The girls, well, "The girls are still complaining about that 40 years later," Dennis laughs.

The Culvers' Mercedes van, fully loaded, with the custom roof racks Dennis had installed. Over its life with the Culvers, the van would take them on three cross-Canada trips as well as countless holiday jaunts all over British Columbia.[22]

Finally, they were ready. Dennis and Eleanor had the Mercedes bus fixed up like a Swiss Army knife on wheels: everyone and every thing had its function and its place. Diefenbaker had been right. The Trans-Canada Highway was about to do for the Culvers exactly what he said it would—bring Canadians together and give this family a chance to reunite its long-separated halves.

But Dief had left a lot out. People have all different kinds of reasons for taking to the highway. Getting together is only one reason people have hit the longest road. The urge to explore the unknown or to flee the known can be equally strong motives to travel. Simple, schedule-free wanderlust can be just as compelling as heading toward a much-anticipated destination. The Trans-Canada gave Canadians 6,440 kilometres (4,000 miles) of blank slate on which to write their own travel stories. The new highway was an empty stage, two lanes wide and a continent long. The dramas that have been played out there have been as different as the desires that have driven them.

These days, Barb Mitchell is an art dealer in Toronto, Ontario, a responsible, articulate, thoughtful, middle-aged woman, content and happy to be part of the community around her. In 1965, however, she was a third-year university student in Vermont with a lot of questions about the world she was about to step into. She was looking for ways to set herself apart, to question the way things were and the boundaries that her parents and her society had drawn around her life.

Barb's feelings were common in her generation. Many of the children born to all those returning soldiers and their new wives during the post-war boom years were asking the same questions. Made increasingly confident by their affluence, education and cultural clout, thousands of young people wanted to break out of what they considered the smug conformity of the 1950s. They wanted spontaneity, not planning; simplicity, not consumer trappings. And for many, breaking out was taken literally. In the thousands, they took to the road, often by the cheapest and most spontaneous method around: riding their thumbs. For a while, it was almost mainstream, a rite of passage for middle-class kids delaying the onset of careers and families. No one can say how many teenagers and young adults in their twenties hitchhiked in the late 1960s and early '70s. No one counted the young people by the shoulder of the Trans-Canada Highway carrying their battered duffels and their signs reading "Anywhere." We're left with memories of informal, rapidly shifting communities of hitchhikers on the highways just outside Canadian cities, lining up and taking turns to flag a ride. And then there are anecdotal reports, such as the one from the Wawa, Ontario, police officer who used to routinely count dozens of young hitchhikers outside of town, lighting small fires to keep warm and keep the blackflies down while they waited for someone to stop. Wawa was such a choke point for hitchhikers—and such a tough place to get a ride from—that for a while the local police association had a fund to help out kids in dire straits.

Not every hitchhiker struggled to thumb their way across Canada. In 1976, a father-and-son team from Vanier, Ontario, may have set some sort of record when they hopped rides from their home all the way to Vancouver and back. They were back on their front porch less than two weeks after leaving it. "It was actually my wife's idea, to help my son and I to bond," says Andrew Lumsden, who was 42 at the time. "She thought a hitchhiking trip across Canada would really help us get to know each other." He and Gavin, 11, barely had time. They reached Vancouver within five days. After three days there, Gavin wanted to come home. "No

In 1965, Barb Mitchell, shown here on the left, was looking to find a kind of freedom that she—and many in her generation—believed could best be found by taking to the road.[23]

reflection on Vancouver, but Gavin was homesick," says Andrew. "Well, he was probably sick of me, actually." The return took a lightning-fast three days. "You've got to look the drivers right in the eye," says Gavin.

Andrew did have an ulterior motive for hitching across Canada, one that had a little more in common with that of some of the young people who had gone before him. In his own way, Andrew wanted the road to bring a little adventure and romance to his life. "Being a chartered accountant, we get ribbed a lot about being very square. That appealed to me, that I could tell my fellow chartered accountants that I hitchhiked across Canada with my son. You know—'What have you done that's interesting? I hitchhiked across Canada.'"

Andrew and Gavin Lumsden, shown here demonstrating their hitching style in a 1975 newspaper photograph, sought to use their time together on the road to build their relationship.[24]

Barb would have understood. "In the 1960s the Trans-Canada was part of the freedom culture of young people," she says. "It was the road that young people wanted to travel. It was the road of adventure. And the kids were hitchhiking up and down, mostly guys. But women were involved in this, too. There were girls that were out there doing things, interacting with this new highway."

Barb wanted to be part of it, to break out herself. That summer she hit the road, catching a ride to Vancouver with two boys she'd met at the American university she attended.

Barb's parents arranged for her and the girlfriend she was travelling with to stay with some family friends once they reached the city. The four travellers got into Vancouver late. Barb didn't want to wake up her parents' friends, who she felt were upright, conservative people who would neither appreciate nor understand the late hour. The young travellers did what seemed like the logical thing and wandered over to Stanley Park, the vast, green space in downtown Vancouver, and bunked down for the night under some bushes. Barb remembers seeing RCMP cruisers prowling around, but she thought they were only there to keep the park safe for people such as herself and her friends. In fact, the police were looking for her at the behest of her parents' friends. When Barb and her girlfriend turned up the next morning, the relief and welcome cooled considerably after the family friends learned how the girls had spent the night. It seemed best to leave, and Barb and her friend were soon off to Victoria, where they spent the rest of the summer. When it was time to go back, they returned to Vancouver, got a couple duffel bags and a sign reading "Eastward," sat down by the side of the Trans-Canada and waited for the next adventure to begin.

The trip was a lark and an adventure, but it was more than that, too. She could have taken the train. After all, Barb's father was a doctor working for Canadian National Railways, and she could have ridden for free anywhere she wanted. But Barb wanted to deliberately flout convention and do something people like her weren't supposed to. For a nice, middle-class girl, sticking her thumb out on the shoulder of the highway was a little bit like sticking it in the eye of polite society. It was rebellious enough that she never did tell her parents that she hitchhiked home. It's no coincidence that the summer Barb hit the road was the same summer she started taking the pill.

"Everything is so free today; everything is permitted. It's hard to explain to people that almost nothing was permitted then," she says. "Young women at that time were kind of feeling their oats, taking up challenges, being able to do what they wanted. Liberation was in the air."

For Barb, the Trans-Canada offered an escape route from conformity and a chance to introduce herself to a world she felt she'd been sheltered from. For others, however, it offered escape of a more immediate, physical kind.

Bonita Garrett is a friendly, loquacious woman who laughs easily and well. She's seen many different sides of life; her resume includes stints as truck driver and abuse counselor. At 52, after two decades of spiritual reflection and search, she's about to be ordained as a full minister of the United Church of Canada and is in line for a master's degree in theology. She's found her mission in helping others, especially abused women. In the summer of 1976, however, she was in an abusive relationship herself, afraid and isolated, knowing her own marriage was sinking lower and growing more dangerous.

Bonita Garrett, shown here about the time she escaped from an abusive marriage, found comfort, safety and independence on the Trans-Canada Highway.[25]

Bonita was then working at Queen's University in Kingston, Ontario, on a three-month contract as a computer technician. At work, it was all lab coats and shiny glassware, mechanical precision and scientific detachment. At home with her alcoholic husband, it was violence, torment and fear. Bonita doesn't recall making the decision to leave. But at one point that summer, she looked around at her beloved antiques—a 150-year-old bentwood rocker, an immaculate, claw-footed Morris chair from the turn of the century—and realized that her treasures would no longer fit into her old Ford Econoline. Something inside her said that maybe it was time for some new wheels.

At an auction sale, Bonita turned up an old army vehicle that had been converted into a bread van. It had three forward gears, a top speed of 65 kilometres (40 miles) per hour, no heater, a steering wheel the size of a basketball hoop and only one seat, but it seemed solid and had plenty of room. She got it for $498, telling her husband it would come in handy if they ever had to move.

She still hadn't decided to leave, for there wasn't much support for abused women in 1976. Domestic violence was still a taboo subject. What happened at home was supposed to remain at home. Battered wives were made to feel that the situation was their fault, and for a while Bonita, too, felt it was her responsibility to try harder.

Her marriage, however, continued to deteriorate. One night, she drove herself in the bread van to the Kingston hospital with cracked ribs and vertebrae. And that autumn, Bonita's husband began to teach himself how to throw knives—not at competition targets or for idle, back-porch amusement, but to hurt people. Soon, Bonita was driving herself to hospital again, this time with a knife wound in her arm from fending off a blade thrown at about chest level. She still has the scar. Finally, she realized it was time to flee.

"I knew that if I didn't leave then, I'd never leave," she says.

Bonita got her chance on December 17, 1976, when her husband left the house to go drinking. She quickly loaded up the van and lumbered out onto the Trans-Canada, headed to her mother's home in Killarney, Manitoba, en route to friends in Kamloops, British Columbia. The night was deadly cold. By the time she hit Kenora, it was −48°C (−54°F). Snowflakes lanced through the yellow cones her headlights threw into the surrounding dark.

With its box-on-wheels styling and top speed of 65 kilometres (40 miles) per hour, Bonita's van wasn't the most glamorous vehicle on the highway. But it took her where she needed to go—into her new life.[26]

All through the night, Bonita trundled along, scraping ice off the inside of the windshield, her dog huddled up as near to the engine block as she could get. Alone and driving over the north shore of Lake Superior, Bonita hit blizzard after blizzard. But somehow she felt much less isolated on the Trans-Canada than she had felt at home.

"I found out who I was on the highway," she says.

"As I left Kingston, there was a tremendous sense of relief. I was on the road, I had packed up everything that I owned and I was safe. And there was a huge sense of almost euphoria. I had packed by myself; it was my vehicle; I had my dog, and I was going to spend Christmas in Killarney. I was going to start a new life with new people in Kamloops. It was almost a high because women weren't supposed to do that. And I was on my way."

Despite the different natures of their trips, Barb and Bonita both hit the road for reasons that have a lot in common. Both had destinations in mind. And both hoped the road would lead them to escape, freedom and, in Bonita's case, even safety. But not everyone travels that way. Many simply like being on the Trans-Canada. They enjoy a life of constant movement. They make the road their job and enjoy the people they meet along the way. One of them is Bob Ridley.

Canada has scores of small-town hockey teams. Some, like those that play in the Western or the Ontario hockey leagues, are so close to the big time that the players can almost imagine their NHL rookie cards. Other leagues are farther removed from the pros. But, whatever their players' prospects of future stardom, they all have two things in common: someone calls the game for the local radio station, and someone drives the Iron Lung, universal junior hockey slang for the team bus. Bob does both.

Bob Ridley has spent a career in sports calling the games on radio and driving the team bus. Year after year, he watches life on the road groom a collection of boys into a team of young men.[27]

In 1968 Bob Ridley arrived in Medicine Hat, Alberta, to call hockey games for the old Medicine Hat Blades, a member of a regional senior league. Bob didn't see many face-offs, however, before the town arena burned down and the team folded. For about a year, Bob did some news and some rock 'n' roll disk jockeying. Then a new arena was built to house a new team playing in a new league, now the WHL. The station manager of CHAT radio asked him if he'd like to be the Voice of the Tigers, and Bob pounced on the opportunity. He did that for two years, calling games both at home and on the road. One day, since he was travelling with the team anyway, management put two and two together and asked him to drive the bus. Bob had grown up on a farm. He was good with machinery and comfortable driving heavy equipment. "Sure," he said. Thirty years and 3.2 million miles (two million miles) later, he's still driving.

"Life on the Trans-Canada's been pretty thrilling for me, actually," he says in the smooth, fluent voice of a broadcaster. "There's always something different each and every time out."

Bob's gotten used to the rhythms of life on the road in the Tigers' bus as it speeds down the highway to Lethbridge or Swift Current or out into British Columbia. There are the dark, silent nights after a loss, when nobody says much and most players just try to get some sleep. There are the raucous post-victory trips, loud with movies and wisecracks. There's a lot of simple time together, talking or doing homework. Sometimes, on stormy nights, the bus will happen upon a driver stranded by the roadside. Bob throws on the brakes, and a busfull of strapping young men pile out, ready and willing to give a push. One night, Bob remembers, the Tigers were the stranded ones. The blizzard was so bad outside of Gull Lake, Saskatchewan, the RCMP closed the Trans-Canada down.

The Tigers headed back into the tiny town, packing the hotel to the rafters. Some players were billeted with local farmers. A couple had to spend the night in jail. Through experiences like that, during the course of a season, the Iron Lung and the Trans-Canada turn a couple dozen individuals into a tight little world of men and boys on the threshold of becoming men. And from the driver's seat of the Tigers' bus, Bob gets an intimate view of young athletes aged 16 to 20 standing on the threshold of their adulthood.

Bob calls the team bus a finishing school for a certain kind of elite. "You learn how to take a loss; you learn how to take a win. You learn what other people are about and how to get along with them. The ups, the downs, the losses, the wins, the pressures from parents, agents, coaches— these kids go through a lot. I have the deepest respect for them. They're very determined, and they're very committed. They don't take a loss easily, and they celebrate when they win." Bob grins, his smooth face suddenly nearly as youthful as the teenagers and twentysomethings around him. "And they're just good, fun people to be around."

A few ex-Tigers—two of the best known being Kelly Hrudey and Lanny Macdonald—have gone on to fame in the National Hockey League. Some have played in Europe, and many more have gone on to college teams in the United States and Canada. Many stay in touch. Every summer, Bob knows he'll get a call from a former defenseman or centre passing through town and wanting to share a cup of coffee with his old companion from his Iron Lung days.

"You don't see them for four or five or maybe even ten years, but eventually you run into them and sit down and talk about old times. That's really special." For Bob Ridley, who's driven the equivalent of eight times to the moon and back, the highway is more than a interlude between two destinations. The movement is the message.

Ed Schmitt knows the road as home, too. He has been working midways all over North America since 1972, setting up and working rides, tearing them down and heading out. Ed's in his fifties now, but his restless energy still fits right in with the whirling arms and garish lights of the carnival rides he trucks from town to town, March through November. He's tried everything from nickel mining to accountancy, but the road is where he found himself.

"You have to be kind of a rebel," he says. "You want to do what really gives you your chance to be yourself. There's less phoniness on the road. I think being here, you're not as phony as, say, working in a store. I mean, you're there, you punch a till, you swipe a card, and to me that's phony. It's not a fun job. This, to me, is a fun job."

After 30 years of it, Ed's got lots of stories about carnival life. These days, he's got a nice, comfortable sleeper cab in his truck, but when he started out, carnies slept wherever they could. Ed has spent nights in tents, under his ride, under his truck, in ticket boxes, barns and laundromats. He's had food poisoning four times from midway food. He laughs describing how he and his buddies used to pick up girls by offering free rounds on the rides and how they used to have contests to see who could pick up the best-looking girl, or sometimes the worst-looking one. "That guy over there," he gestures, striding down the midway in Lethbridge, Alberta, "he showed me everything there is to know about running gambling games, how to take people's money so they didn't quite understand what we were doing." He laughs his booming laugh again.

As Ed sees it, his job is to be an entertainer. He and his fellow carnies create a world of sound and sensation separate from the everyday. Rides

The travelling, nomadic life of a carnie is where Ed Schmitt found himself. Everything else, he says, felt "phony."[28]

and games offer adults a little bit of risk and adventure. Crowds and darkness offer the young a little anonymity they can use to create a world of their own, apart, for a night, from their parents.

The nighttime world of the carnival combines garish lights and the invisibility of darkness and crowds—an allure that keeps the crowds coming even in the age of virtual reality video games.[29]

But providing other people's fun can be hard work. Turnaround time, from teardown and transport to setup, can be as short as 12 hours. And Ed's $1.1 million ride, the Spin Out, takes a lot of maintenance. It's not unusual for him to change 700 light bulbs in one morning. But the carnival and the road, 32,000 kilometres (20,000 miles) of it a year, answer all his wants. Even Ed's girlfriend, Debbie, works down the midway at the candy floss booth.

Ed recalls how, when he was a kid, his mother used to take him to carnivals. Surrounded by the swirling, flashing lights, the rush and press of crowds, the shouts and music and smells, he would get happily lost. Today, nearly half a decade later, a grown man, he's still lost in the carnival.

"I've been here 31 years and I'll probably be here until they put me in a box," he says. "It's a thing that grows on you—just the feeling that you're going to a different place and you're just travelling. That's it."

Musician Bucky Adams has also been travelling the Trans-Canada most of his adult life. For him, a taste for the travelling life is as natural as a feel for rhythm.

"Music just seems to come to me when I'm driving the road," says Bucky, who's been playing jazz from city to city all over the Maritimes since well before the Trans-Canada was built. "It seems like music and driving on the highway go together. I've composed a few songs on the highway also. It's just natural for me. I can be driving along and all of a sudden I'll start singing. Maybe it's the wide open spaces, the freedom. I wouldn't do it on the normal streets, but on the highway it's just a good feeling."

It's a feeling Bucky, who plays trumpet and saxophone, has known all his life. His parents were also musicians and entertainers, playing vaudeville and dance halls as far back as the 1900s. Bucky played his first professional gig in 1948 at the age of 11, with the Barnum and Bailey Circus. It wasn't long before he was leading his own band and living the life he's known ever since. Halifax, Sydney, Cape Breton, New Glasgow, Truro, as far west as Vancouver—anywhere there's a bandstand, there's Bucky. He hasn't gotten rich, but he's shared the stage with musicians like Louis Armstrong and Dizzy Gillespie. Duke Ellington wrote a tune for Bucky's wife. And he still loves the road.

For Bucky Adams, music and the Trans-Canada are intertwined. Not only does the road take him from gig to gig, it also inspires him to create new sounds.[30]

"Every band I've ever had, it's like the family going on the road. We'd be singing in the car, we'd be talking, we'd have so much fun we'd get to where we were going and didn't realize we'd been out there a long time. I can't wait to get on the road and go play. When somebody calls me up for a job, I don't care where it's at. We'll get in the car and go. The boys can't wait for me to call.

"It's a jazz musician's pleasure. It's a pleasure to get on the highway and just go. Stop and play some music and go again."

For some, the road is a link between people in far-flung communities. For some, it's a way to break links that have grown too confining. For some, the road itself is enough. But there is another group of travellers who head down the highway in search of no earthly destination. The Trans-Canada has seen its share of spiritual travellers, people who see in its black and gritty asphalt the promise of a shining path.

In 1974 Allan Kelly and Donna McVeigh were living in Montreal and slowly falling in love. But as they tried to imagine together how their future lives would look, they began to realize how unhappy they were with their present ones. Allan, then 33, a black-bearded bear of a man, was in his 13th year as a delivery driver for Eaton's department store. Donna, a petite, long-haired brunette with an open, innocent face, was just turning 19 and hadn't done much of anything yet. Both knew, however, that city life—fighting traffic, fighting noise, fighting congestion and collapsing at the end of the day in front of the TV—was not how they wanted to spend their lives. Allan's first thought was to sell everything, buy a Harley-Davidson motorcycle and head south toward the sun. But after his bills were paid, the money he got for his car, his furniture and everything else he sold wasn't enough for the big bike. So with the fearlessness of youth,

The Longest Road

Donna looked at him and said, "It's warm in British Columbia. Why don't we buy a couple horses and travel to B.C. on them?" Allan couldn't think of a reason why not. There was no reason to hurry, nothing awaiting them at the end of the trip. And approached with the right attitude, the trip itself might lead toward the escape they both craved.

In 1974, Donna Kelly was ready for anything and her youthful optimism and confidence swept Allan along on their horseback adventure.[31]

Donna had some experience on horseback. Allan had none at all. His co-workers at Eaton's laughed at him; his ex-wife worried that he was abandoning his two sons. Donna's parents feared for their safety. But Donna's zest for the adventure invigorated Allan, made him feel alive in a way he hadn't for years. "I wanted to be with her and all this enthusiasm," he recalls. "It had been a lot of years I'd been sitting on my butt not doing anything. I wanted to take her energy and put it into mine. It was great. And I needed it."

There wasn't a lot of planning; they'd eat when they got hungry, sleep when they got tired in a tent they'd pitch by the roadside. Sixty-five kilometres (40 miles) a day shouldn't be a problem, they thought. Pictures taken at the start of the trip show them dressing the trail-rider part: boots, cowboy hats, fringed leather jackets, even a gun in a holster. "Love and common sense," Donna says. "That's what we figured we'd travel on."

But the two laugh now at how green they were. Allan and Donna both took a few spills until they figured out that the leather strap around the horse's midriff that keeps the saddle upright stretches during the course of a day's ride and needs to be periodically tightened. Their naivety even cost them their original mounts. Outside of Ottawa, one of their two pintos developed a limp. It was just a stone bruise and would have been fine in few days, but Allan and Donna thought it much more serious. They asked the owner of a local ranch for advice, who told them that the pinto's travelling days were over. Lucky for them, he had an old wagon horse and a rig he'd swap for the pintos. Not knowing any better, Allan and Donna agreed. And that's how they continued their trip, sitting up on a covered wagon behind old Lucky, like a couple of modern-day homesteaders, heading west just like in the movies. By the end of summer, they thought

After trading away their riding horses, the Kellys were to spend the next weeks travelling, eating and sleeping in this covered wagon, pulled by old Lucky, the horse.[32]

Colleen Deschamps, who drove from coast to coast living in her car, was another traveller who used the road to cut herself off from her former life in order to imagine a better one.[33]

they'd be in Victoria, where their believed their new lives awaited them. They had a lot to learn, and the road was about to teach them.

Colleen Deschamps is an alumnus of the same asphalt classroom. She's about 20 years younger than Donna, but the two have much in common. They were both about the same age when they hit the Trans-Canada, looking for something they couldn't quite name. At 17 Colleen decided that she, too, wanted a break from her life to give some thought to how to live a better one.

Like Donna and Allan, Colleen needed simplicity. She needed to dial out the white noise of her regular job, her friends, her family and her routine, and the road seemed a good place for that. One day in 1996 she decided it was time to head out. Colleen called up her friend Rachel and asked her if she wanted to drive with her from Penticton, British Columbia, across the country. There would be no agenda, just a few pins in the map marking places they were curious about or towns where they had friends. If they couldn't find a bed for the night, they'd just sleep in their car. "I was really seeking God at that time in my life," Colleen says. "It was for me a faith journey, just seeing where everything led. Seeing where we would wind up geographically, emotionally, physically and spiritually. And the Trans-Canada Highway was a way for us to leave where we were from and get somewhere else."

They cooked four-course meals right in the front seat of Colleen's Ford Tempo. First, she'd get a little hot water from a convenience store, using it to heat up some instant rice in a soup base. They'd eat the rice, then put in some wheat thins and eat those. The instant noodle course would follow, finished off by slurping the juice.

"Living in your car changes your whole mindset," she says. "It's so free living in your car. There's nothing tying you down. You have no responsibilities. It was a really good time for me to connect with God because life was so simple."

Without Colleen knowing it, another Trans-Canada pilgrim was setting off that same summer in search of the same kind of grace. Bhaktimarga Swami is a Hindu monk, a sannyasi, one who has chosen a life of renunciation. Bhaktimarga came to Krishna Consciousness in 1972 as a 20-year-old fine arts student at a school in Sudbury. One day he was walking home from class when he saw a group of young men standing by the Trans-Canada, chanting and drumming. Bhaktimarga had been raised a Catholic, but he no longer felt at home in his spiritual culture and was searching for something new. The young men by the road aroused his curiosity. That night Bhaktimarga invited them home to his apartment, and his new spiritual path had begun. By 1996 he was living in a monastery, his life devoted to his beliefs. Life in the ashram, however, was growing increasingly busy. Time to reflect was scarce. That year was also the centenary of the birth of Srila Prabhupada, one of Bhaktimarga's teachers and inspirations, and he wanted to do something special to honour it. The answer came to him in the name he was given when he was ordained as a monk: *Bhaktimarga* means "path of devotion." The idea of pilgrimage, a holy journey undertaken to remove oneself from normal life to focus on spiritual matters, plays a prominent role in many eastern religions. Bhaktimarga decided he would adapt this ancient practice from his adopted culture to the country of his birth. He had already travelled the Trans-Canada by bus and by hitchhiking; this time, he would do it up close by walking its entire length west to east, facing the rising sun. Walking would be the best way to open a channel for whatever experience or wisdom might offer itself, he thought. At night he would sleep in the battered 1976 Dodge van driven by a friend who was backing him up. But otherwise, he would live simply along the roadside, napping under trees, accepting whatever charity was offered, chanting his beads as he went and writing in his journal. He would be nobody but himself, with a monk's traditional saffron robes and shaved head. His only concession was to drop sandals for several pairs of sturdy runners. "I wanted to do it up close where I could really get to see the plants, the stones, to meet the people and be exposed and be myself," Bhaktimarga says. "And go in my traditional robe and just be who I am and let occur whatever is to occur."

For Bhaktimarga Swami, who walked from coast to coast, the Trans-Canada Highways was both a path for his feet and a path for his soul.[34]

Bhaktimarga's spiritual journey had begun on the Trans-Canada Highway, where the course of his religious life was changed. And it was to the highway that he returned. On April 12, 1996, he faced the Pacific Ocean in Victoria, said a prayer, dabbed his forehead with seawater, turned around and began walking. "These legs were made for that particular purpose," says Bhaktimarga. "Walking really generates a sense of reflection and gaining focus. Because I was doing the most simple of things, after the walk I could remember details very, very clearly. And it was meditative, too. What was I meditating on? Just getting the job done and performing my duty, which was walking."

CHAPTER 4

After six months of planning, modifying their bus and sleeping with maps, the Culvers were finally ready to hit the road on June 26, 3:00 P.M. sharp. There was a plan for every day, which included D-day, or departure day. But actually getting out of the driveway turned out to be more complicated than expected.

The upcoming trip had been the subject of much conversation at Dennis's office, and one of his secretaries passed the story along to her roommate. That roommate worked at one of Vancouver's newspapers, and when word spread among the city's reporters, it seemed every media outlet in town wanted to do a feature on the ultimate family road trip. The newspapers were easily accommodated—an interview, a couple of still photos posed by the bus. But the TV crew from the CBC wanted to actually film the Culvers hitting the road. That didn't sound too intrusive, and everyone agreed. Even better, the Culvers were informed they'd be on the six o'clock news that night. That meant if they got away in time, they could stop in at Abbotsford and watch the news at a friend's house.

Departure plans proceeded as anticipated. The night before D-day, Dennis loaded the heavy boxes onto the roof rack, covered them with a tarp and roped everything down. After he left for work the next morning, Eleanor was to pack and load the suitcases, bake some bread for sandwiches and get the kids ready. At 3:00 P.M. on the dot, she was to drive the bus over to the office. Dennis would hop in, suit and all, and off they'd go. As far as Dennis knew, that was exactly what was happening—until Eleanor called. "Every time I try to pack something," she said, "the TV people say that's interesting, Mrs. Culver, that's good color. Would you mind unpacking it and doing it again so we could film it?" Even with two housekeepers hired to mind the children and clean the house, Eleanor was falling behind schedule. With all the packing and repacking and smiling for the camera, it wasn't until after four o'clock that Eleanor got away, the final moment, a roll of toilet paper bouncing out the door of the bus and unraveling down the street, faithfully caught on film.

When Eleanor picked him up, Dennis knew they weren't going make Abbotsford by news time. "Watch for a TV antenna," he instructed as they drove. When one was spotted, Dennis pulled over, the family trooped up to the doorstep, rang the bell and Eleanor asked the strangers if they minded if she and her family took over their living room to watch themselves on TV. Perhaps too surprised to do anything else, the young couple agreed. The Culvers caught the news just in time, watched the toilet paper roll tumble downhill once again, thanked their benefactors, and headed out. The Culvers were on their way, just slightly behind schedule.

Down the Trans-Canada they went, following the path of the old Cariboo Road up the Fraser River, retracing the tracks of the old stage-coaches and gold dust-laden mule trains. All night long the Mercedes diesel rumbled through the mountains, and sometime during that first 17-hour stretch, the Culvers crossed the Continental Divide at the Rogers Pass.

That they were able to drive the pass literally in their sleep is a tribute to the engineers who built it. While the highway over the Rogers is one of the most scenic stretches of mountain road anywhere, it was also one of the most difficult to build in the entire Trans-Canada—and at $1 million a mile, one of the most expensive.

Tom Matheson was an inspecting engineer for the province of Manitoba in 1957, working on the Trans-Canada project as the liaison between Ottawa and the provincial governments of Manitoba and Saskatchewan.

Road-building on the prairies had its challenges. Manitoba's infamous gumbo soil turned into the worst kind of sucking muck when it rained. In Saskatchewan, crews had to deal with the blizzards. In fact, the last eight

Tom Matheson, a natural builder, found construction of the Rogers Pass section of the Trans-Canada to be the greatest and most inspiring challenge of his life.[35]

kilometres (five miles) of the Trans-Canada through Saskatchewan were paved on October 31, 1957, just two hours before the onslaught of a howler of a snowstorm that would have piled up the drifts, frozen the soil and shut the work down until April.

But generally, rolling out the highway over the prairies was pretty straightforward. "You cut and fill, cut and fill," says Tom. That has a lot to do with why Saskatchewan's section of the road was the first one finished.

Crews such as this 1954 group outside Swift Current, Saskatchewan, found the main challenges of prairie roadbuilding were mainly weather-related. Rain turned soil to muck and
early blizzards could shut construction down for the season.[36]

Wherever there's a road to open, there's a politician with a pair of scissors. Here, then-pre-
mier Tommy Douglas does the honours for Saskatchewan's section of the Trans-Canada at
Regina in August, 1957.[37]

Tom, however, was about to be offered the chance to tackle something
a little more challenging. As he surveyed Manitoba's Riding Mountain
National Park, Tom had gotten to know some of the Parks Canada staff,
including some of the engineers from Banff. When he was finished his
highway on the plains, they asked if he'd be interested in taking charge of
a section through the Rogers Pass.

Tom Matheson is a natural builder. Even after retirement, he couldn't
stop building, and with no more roads to construct, he built himself a
2,000 square foot log cabin on a Manitoba lake, complete with deck and
swimming pool. Tom loves to watch things come together, the bigger the

better, and when he got the offer to work in the British Columbia mountains, he didn't hesitate. "I didn't have to think it over very long," he says.
"It was a real challenge. I knew this was going to be completely different,
and I said 'Yeah, I'll give it a whirl.' And I never regretted it one bit. It was
exciting. It was a challenge every day."

Tom was placed in charge of the ten kilometres (six miles) of highway
right at the top of the pass. It was as daunting a task as any Canadian engineer has ever faced. The Rogers Pass wasn't quite untouched wilderness—
the road would use the same right-of-way as the CPR—but it was remote
and rugged. Its position at 1,325 metres (4,000 feet) of elevation right on

the Continental Divide subjected it to about 8.5 metres (28 feet) of snow a year, one of the highest averages in Canada. And on either side of the pass, peaks stretch 3,050 kilometres (10,000 feet) into the sky. Put the two together and you've got prime country for crushing, killing avalanches. In fact, the Rogers Pass used to be known as the Death Pass because of all the railway workers who had been carried off by rockslides and avalanches along its length. A total of 236 workers over 30 years were killed before the CPR finally gave up trying to keep its tracks clear and built the eight-kilometre (five-mile) Connaught Tunnel.

But despite danger and difficulty, the road had to be built. The old Big Bend Highway simply wasn't good enough for trucks and other commercial traffic, and if a proper road wasn't punched through the mountains, the worth of the whole Trans-Canada Highway would be reduced. By the time Tom agreed to take on the project, a team of engineers, scientists and Swiss snow experts were already roaming the high country, often on skis, trying to come up with ways to keep snow and rock from roaring down the steep slopes, wiping out the highway and its travellers.

Tom got out to his section of the road for the 1960 summer construction season, and he wasn't long on the site before he realized the magnitude of his task. There was the unpredictable mountain weather, of course. Surveyors struggled to get accurate readings through snow piled three metres (ten feet) deep that lasted for weeks and weeks. Some days, crews woke to find themselves right in the middle of low-hanging clouds, making it impossible to take any sightings. Weeks of rain would wash down landslides and soak everybody's clothes for days at a time. But the biggest challenge was simply the unforgiving alpine terrain.

Mountain roadbuilders had to work around all kinds of obstacles, from steep cliffsides to tight curves to rushing streams coursing over the rock. Ingenuity was an essential part of their tool kit.[38]

In the prairies, a tight curve could be smoothed just by buying a little more land. In the high country, engineers had to build gradual curves and gentle grades using only what the mountains gave them. To make matters worse, the CPR had already taken the easiest grades and the few level spots; the highway builders had to make the best of what was left. Blasting

These innovative, sturdy snow sheds being built along the Rogers Pass would keep the highway open most of the year, but even they haven't been able to fully tame that area's notorious avalanches. Most winters, the Trans-Canada still loses a few days, buried under snow shed by the surrounding mountains.[39]

away the stubborn rock was often the only way to clear a path, but that made for slow progress. It could take days to clear away the rubble from a single blast. Sometimes, explosions would open up an underground spring and the road would be awash. In all, it took 5,000 tonnes of explosives to get through the Selkirks. And when it wasn't rock, it was muskeg, as deep as 18 metres (60 feet). "There was no level playing field," Tom recalls.

Sometimes, Tom's crew had to try things nobody had done before. In July 1960, repeated landslides were blocking one curve along the route. The more crews tried to dig the road out, the more rock slid down to cover their efforts. In a solid week of work, they cleared less than six metres (20 feet) of road. Tom needed to step back and get an overview of the problem, so he hitched a ride on a freight train coming through the pass and asked the engineer to slow down as he passed the troublesome spot. He discovered that the slide was coming from a giant horseshoe of loose soil and rock about 245 metres (800 feet) up the slope from the road that got bigger all the time as more rubble tumbled down. When Tom saw that, he knew they could dig for 20 years and the slides would still be coming. The highway would have to hang off the side of the mountain, he decided. First, crews dug out as much as they could without bringing down more rock, which left them about six metres (20 feet) short of the width they'd need for the curve. Then they ordered a giant metal bin, built to the exact specifications of the curve, and bolted it to the side of the mountain with giant rods. They filled the bin with sand and built the highway over top of it.

Meanwhile, the avalanche control experts had been busy. Engineers decided to build three levels of defense. The first used an old trick adapted from the Second World War. Workers dotted likely avalanche slopes

Although this bridge is being built over Banff National Park's Nigel Creek, not the Rogers Pass, this 1960 photograph gives a pretty good idea of why building the Trans-Canada over the Rockies was one of the hardest, slowest and most expensive parts of the longest road.[40]

with 170 so-called dragon's teeth—cone-shaped concrete hills 3.5–7.5 metres (12–25 feet) high—originally developed to block the advance of enemy tanks. The dragon's teeth would slow and break up onrushing snow. Then, they pushed up earthen embankments three metres (ten feet) high and up to 45 metres (150 feet) long to both limit the size of avalanches and to divert their flow away from the road. Finally, they designed the famous snow sheds—concrete and steel tunnels over the highway built to withstand 545 kilograms (1,200 pounds) per square inch of pressure.

On top of all that, they instituted a system of avalanche control using carefully aimed artillery fire to bring down snow slabs before they got too big. The control systems work—most of the time. In spite of the engineers' best efforts, however, the mountains aren't completely tamed, and avalanches still close the Rogers Pass periodically, especially toward spring, as the warming sun heats up and destabilizes the top layers of the snowpack.

In the prairies, a good team in a hurry could survey up to eight kilometres (five miles) of road route a day. In the mountains, Tom found that 30 metres (100 feet) of progress was a good day. In the prairies, roadbuilders could lay more than 100 metres (325 feet) of asphalt a day. A good day's work in the Rogers Pass might result in six metres (20 feet) of new roadbed. Ten kilometres (six miles) of prairie highway was three months work at most. The Rogers Pass was to take five years.

"Our boys had a pretty good vision, and it worked," Tom says, his big strong hands and blunt features growing animated as he talks about the greatest challenge he ever faced. "Everybody that went in there was confident. They were going to build a highway—it didn't matter. You know, you can send a Canadian in anywhere in the world and they'll build whatever."

For five years during the construction of the Rogers Pass section of the highway, workers spent summers in isolated, rough-and-ready construction camps like this one.[41]

It was exciting, challenging work, but it was isolated. Hundreds of workers and subcontractors lived in a camp near the construction site: two dorms, a dining hall, a building for toilets, showers and laundry, and a general office. Tom had his own quarters. There was no phone and no radio. The railway's telegraph line was the only connection to the outside world. Fortunately, the camp was a congenial place full of lively personalities. Tom remembers an Australian surveyor, an ex-British Army draftsman, a champion skier from Banff, a chef from the Banff Springs Hotel, and workers from Ottawa, the prairies and other places in Canada.

"We had lots of things in common," says Tom. "We had a baseball diamond we made down in the river flats. We tried to play football but we didn't have enough equipment, and too many guys got hurt. We had some pretty good bridge players. Quite a few of the boys used to do mountain climbing. And every time the contractor blasted rock, everybody went in there to see if there was any gold showing up."

Tom's summer was lit up by the visit of his wife and eight-year-old daughter, Melanie. For Melanie, that visit has remained a highlight of her life.

"Mother and I were a diversion, so I was treated like a princess. I really was," Melanie says. For her arrival, the chef made an enormous cake with purple icing. But the best part was watching the construction. Melanie, now an artist, has clear memories of how it looked.

"I like watching construction because there's a pattern and a rhythm to the work. And to watch people doing what they love doing is wonderful. They were excited about what they were accomplishing—all of them. It didn't matter whether they were hucking rock or driving a Cat or supervising, they were loving it, and they worked as a team. Even as a little kid I could see that."

And at the centre of it all was her daddy—"this big guy who do anything," says Melanie. Her admiration for her father intensified as she watched him running the show.

"And it was even more so when I was there because he was in charge," she recalls. "They were all doing stuff that was exciting and big. Everything was huge. The mountain was huge. The machines were huge. Everything is on a really grand scale when you're on top of the world, and that's what it feels like when you're up at Rogers Pass. It feels like being on top of the world, and I got to live there and watch my dad build this road.

Building the Rogers Pass highway brought together hundreds of men from all over Canada, such as this unidentified worker. Tom Matheson remembers off-hours spent in baseball games, epic card tournaments and exploring the mountains.[42]

"I still feel like that when I go there. When I drive through the Pass, I'm a little kid again, and I say 'My dad built this.' It's our road."

That summer on top of the world gave Tom some of his favourite memories and proudest moments.

"It was really something," he says. "I never realized it to start with, but to me it was just the finest thing in the world. I'll never get another chance to build something like that again. Never ever. Being the first to do it was really something. It's just like a hockey player winning the Stanley Cup. That's how it felt. Really, really good."

CHAPTER 5

NOT QUITE TWO DAYS INTO THEIR JOURNEY, THE CULVERS HIT THEIR FIRST speed bump. Sometime as they crossed the mountains, something got into their food. Something bad.

Despite the departure delay, things had been going well, too—exactly according to plan. The only hitch had been easily overcome. Eleanor had forgotten to stow a knife handy and had no way to spread butter on the lunch sandwiches, so Dennis pulled the key from the ignition (which on that vehicle didn't kill the engine), and Eleanor used that. Problem solved. And right on schedule, the Culvers supped in the Kananaskis area on the edge of the Alberta Rockies and headed out onto the plains west of Calgary, the sun setting over the purple mountains behind them.

That's when the first child started vomiting. With Eleanor asleep, the role of nurse fell to daughter Margo, then eight years old, who was sitting in the co-pilot's seat. Crawling into the passenger area, Margo located a jerry can of water, mopped up the mess and cleaned up her younger sister's face. Unfortunately, there was to be more than one victim. Over the next 17 hours, as the bus trundled along beneath the nighttime prairie skies of Alberta and Saskatchewan, every single Culver fell prey to cramps and nausea, with the sole exceptions being Dennis and Margo.

"It was distressing, but there was nothing to do but keep going," says Dennis. They couldn't just stop at a pharmacy. They were in the middle of nowhere, and it was the middle of the night. So Dennis kept driving, and Margo kept heading into the back with kind words, gentle hands, clean towels and cool water. Finally, the bedraggled and queasy Culvers pulled into their rest stop at Brandon, Manitoba. Although eating was on the schedule, nobody much felt like it. Even Dennis and Margo, after 17 hours in a rolling hospital ward, were starting to feel a bit green. Fortunately, the next stop, only six hours away, was in Winnipeg. There, the Vancouver Culvers were able to pause at the home of Dennis' brother and sister-in-law, Gerald and Di Culver. The chance to get properly cleaned up and relax for an hour or two in a real bed went a long way toward restoring everyone's travelling spirit. The trip resumed—on schedule.

The Trans-Canada Highway did much to open up northern Ontario, but the drive across the Shield was still a long, lonely one. This couple just outside Wawa in the early '60s may have been checking their map to see if they had enough gas to make it to the next town.[43]

Still, the incident made one fact as clear as the white line down the middle of the road: in 1963, driving the Trans-Canada was a pretty lonely thing to do. There weren't many services along the route. In fact, Mercedes-Benz of Canada felt it necessary to provide the owners of its vehicles with a booklet detailing all the stations where diesel was available. "There was nothing on the highway to speak of in those days in the way of facilities," says Dennis. "The tourist industry hadn't really matured along the road. Travelling it was quite an adventure." But that was rapidly changing. Wherever the road went, or wherever twisting, single-lane gravel was transformed into smooth blacktop, Canada opened up.

Few parts of the country were more in need of opening up than northern Ontario. The Canadian Shield had frustrated travellers from the days of the earliest explorers. Getting through it was still a tough go even by the end of the Second World War—especially the 260 kilometres (160 miles) between Marathon and the Agawa River. Although a road farther north through the Shield had been completed in 1946, communities on the north shore of Lake Superior had to depend on water or rail transport. They had no road at all. In 1957 Tony Dias became one of the men charged with closing that gap.

Tony was born and raised in East Africa, then moved to England to study engineering. After working for a couple years in Devon, he heard of an intriguing offer from the Government of Canada. Canadian universities weren't graduating enough engineers to build the public works the growing country needed, so the government was shopping for engineers abroad. Tony applied and was accepted. They told him he'd be building highways, and Tony pictured himself in a white shirt and tie, sitting in an office lined with maps, charts and blueprints. Instead, he found himself living in a bush camp—a half-dozen trailers, a cookshack, outhouse and a bathing shed—somewhere between Kenora and Dryden. This is where he would spend the next 18 months. A picture from those days hints at Tony's displacement. There he is—a slightly built, carefully groomed young man with dark hair and piercing eyes, puffing thoughtfully at a pipe. A glass of sherry in his hand wouldn't have looked out of place. Outside the door of the roughhewn Canadian bunkhouse, however, was no green and pleasant land but the raw, rugged wilderness of northern Ontario.

Despite the pleasure of his friend's music, Tony, shown here on the left, remembers his early days in the bush camps of northern Ontario as lonely, hard and not at all what he'd grown used to in England.[44]

"One Saturday I was alone in camp doing my laundry," Tony recalls in his precise, English-educated voice. "I'd pulled the old wringer washer out onto the porch of the kitchen and gone back for a pail with hot water to fill the tub and there was a bear standing directly across the washing machine in front of me. I was six months out of Britain. What the heck was this bear doing across from me? There was nowhere to run. So I gently moved backwards with the hot pail of water in my hand and opened the kitchen door and slid back inside."

Tony compares his work to a tailor adapting a universal pattern to an individual body. Overall plans were sent down from head office, and his job was to make them work and fit them to actual conditions on the ground. Those actual conditions gave Tony the toughest challenge he'd ever faced. The land was so inaccessible that heavy machinery had to be barged in over Lake Superior or even flown in by helicopter. To push a road through the dense granite of the Shield—some of the oldest, hardest rock on earth—workers blasted cuts up to 185 metres (600 feet) long and 25 metres (75 feet) deep. Twenty-five major bridges had to be erected, one of them 180 metres (590 feet) long. The muskeg was so treacherous that equipment left out overnight might be gone by morning. Engineers avoided bogs when they could. But when they couldn't, trenches up to three metres (ten feet) deep and 120 metres (400 feet) long had to be dug in the spongy muck, then filled with rock, gravel and sand. The consequences of sloppy work were quick and catastrophic. One night, muskeg swallowed three kilometres (two miles) of road that had just been completed that day.

Conditions for the men were tough. Work kept up all winter, in temperatures that dipped to –46°C (–50°F). In the summer, the only way to shower was to take a bucket down to the river, batting at the inevitable clouds of blackflies. The lakes were full of leeches. And for a stranger in a strange, new land, it was often lonely.

The stubborn rock of the Canadian Shield was a constant challenge to road construction crews, as shown in this 1953 photo between Bigwood and Rutter, Ontario. Just to stake out a route, this worker needed a pneumatic drill to punch into the granite.[45]

"I didn't make very many friends," Tony recalls. "There were many, many weekends in those 18 months that I spent by myself. My first Christmas was spent in a bush camp all by myself. My first New Year's was in a bush camp all by myself. I can remember buying a bottle of Scotch and sitting on my bunk bed on New Year's Eve, drinking a few glasses. I think the thing that kept me going was that I was supporting my mother, who lived in England. I felt an obligation to continue doing that, but I also felt that I'd made a decision."

Many times he thought about quitting and looking for easier work in another province or the United States. But his conviction that he should see through what he had begun kept him at it, and eventually things began to look up. Marriage in 1959 to a woman he met in Dryden eased his loneliness. The following year, the Trans-Canada Highway over Lake Superior was complete. And somehow, the years of isolation, hard work and achievement turned Tony into a Canadian.

"When I look back on my own national identity, I had none," he says. "I was born in East Africa of East Indian and French parentage. I was a British subject, but I was not English. When I became a Canadian citizen in 1962, my national identity was defined. I hadn't realized it until I travelled out west. Driving across the prairies gave me a sense of what Canada really meant to me. The vastness of the country, the pioneering spirit, the sacrifices that the early immigrants made in the opening up of the country demonstrated a spirit of wanting to belong, a pioneer spirit. In a very, very small sense, my adventures in Kenora allowed me to relate to that. The fact that I had put up with hardships allowed me to relate on a very small scale to what I believe to be the experiences of the people who opened up the west—the oriental people who built the railway, the homesteaders who went out to the farms. My experience with the Trans-Canada Highway helped me to later identify with what it meant to be a Canadian. I'm proud to have found my national identity in that."

The work of Tony Dias and men like him had an immediate effect on northern Ontario. Howard Whent, a proud local historian who still lives in the area, saw them first-hand. Howard grew up in the town of White River, right in the middle of the roadless gap between Marathon and Agawa Bay. White River was on the main line of the Canadian Pacific

Tony Dias—East Africa-born, British-educated, Canadian by dint of his experience building the Trans-Canada Highway.[46]

The line-up to be among the first to drive the Trans-Canada over Lake Superior stretched far into the distance the day the road opened. This is only the start of a queue that was 4,000 cars long.[47]

Railway, and when Howard was a boy that was how most people got in and out of town. The only other choice was to take a boat down Lake Superior to Sault Ste. Marie. Either way, says Howard, it was not a short trip. Nobody said "Let's go for a drive." There was nowhere to drive to. The folks in White River, however, were better off than those in Wawa, just 100 kilometres (60 miles) south, where there was only a branch line. Getting out of Wawa required taking a local train, then waiting a day or two for the next connection. Although Wawa and White River were so close, Howard says their isolation from each other was so complete that they hardly knew each other existed.

Howard was about ten years old when the highway crews pushed east from Marathon into White River. Overnight, it was the fascination and fixation of every boy in town. Every night after school, they'd ride their bikes as far up and down the new road as they could. And at Christmas, boys weren't asking for steam trains any more. It was graders and dump trucks they wanted. The pent-up demand for a road was so great that local people were using the temporary construction roads well before the highway was complete. One winter night, Howard's family did just that to drive into Marathon. Marathon had a TV signal, and Howard and his family were able to watch the 1960 Montreal Canadiens on their march to the Stanley Cup.

The link over Lake Superior was officially opened on September 17, 1960. Despite the drizzly weather, almost the entire town of Wawa turned out and 4,000 cars lined up behind the ribbon to be among the first to drive the new highway. By the summer of 1961, it was serving 3,000 vehicles a day. Towns along its path were never the same again. Wawa opened three hotels, six service stations, two gift shops, a general store, a drugstore and a bank within the first year of the Trans-Canada's opening. About 800 cars were sold in a town of 4,000 people. And the town fathers commissioned the Wawa goose, perhaps the first of the giant monuments that now punctuate the Trans-Canada drive. *Wawa* is Ojibway for "wild goose." The giant plaster and steel-mesh bird was intended to lure tourists off the highway into the business strip. It seems to have worked. Howard says the adjacent visitors' centre gets between 60,000 and 80,000 visitors a year.

Perhaps the most famous of the giant landmarks that punctuate the Trans-Canada, the Wawa goose has succeeded admirably in drawing tourists off the road and into the town.[48]

In northern Ontario, the Trans-Canada was like a giant power cord, allowing the region to plug into the rest of the world. Montreal was far from an isolated wilderness, but it, too, received a jolt of energy from the highway. The city had been connected to the rest of the country since the fur trade days when it was the terminus of the old canoe brigades, and the beginning of the 1960s saw the island at the city's centre served by two bridges and a number of roads. But that infrastructure was from an earlier day. The old two-lane Jacques Cartier Bridge dated from the early 1900s, and the Victoria Bridge was even older. And in many ways, the aging transportation infrastructure was a reflection of the province's social foundations. For decades, Quebec had been a relative social and political backwater. It had grown along with the rest of the country, but had not modernized. Now, at last, Quebec's horizons were expanding along with its economy and population. The province was beginning to stir and look outside its boundaries at its role in the country and the world. Change was overdue—in more ways than traffic control.

In 1960 Quebec voters tossed out Maurice Duplessis' old Union Nationale government in favour of the Liberals led by Jean Lesage. Lesage realized that if Quebec was to move forward, among the first things it needed would be modern, safe, direct highways. He wasted little time. His first year in office, Lesage signed the federal Trans-Canada Highway Act, the last premier to do so. Part of the deal for the Quebec portion of the Trans-Canada was to include a new, modern road link into Montreal. Ideas and plans were debated for two years, until Lesage was re-elected under the slogan *Maitres chez nous*—"Masters in Our Own House." That phrase kicked off the renaissance of Quebec nationalism and the changing of the province's entire social structure. Those changes became known as the Quiet Revolution. That same year, work began on the Louis-Hippolyte La Fontaine Bridge Tunnel, a new link to the old city worthy of a modern metropolis. Roger Nicolet, a young engineer barely out of school, was chosen to coordinate the entire project.

Roger Nicolet, coordinating engineer of the Louis-Hippolyte La Fontaine Bridge Tunnel, believes that the enormous, innovative project was both a symbol of and a catalyst for Quebec's growing confidence in the early 1960s.[49]

The bridge tunnel would be not only modern, but would be positively bold. Roger's team wanted to move traffic quickly, reliably and safely without scarring long-established neighbourhoods. The plan was to build a bridge to an island halfway across the St. Lawrence, then an underwater tunnel the rest of the way into the city. Conventional engineering, however, wouldn't work. A tunnel through the muddy bottom of the St. Lawrence would simply collapse, and the bedrock was too deep underground to tunnel through.

Innovation was required. Roger's team decided to try a technique that had only been used once before, and then only on a much smaller scale. They planned to cast the tunnel in enormous concrete sections, float them into position, sink them into a trench on the riverbed, and join them underwater. The budget, more than $84 million for less than a mile of tunnel and approaches, would be as grand as the design. "It was experimental at best," says Roger. "It hadn't really been tried before."

But it worked. And in its success, Roger says the bridge tunnel became more than just another public works project. Its scale and boldness made it both a symbol and a cause of the new, confident, outward-looking spirit of Quebec. "In a successful project, in the course of its construction, it develops a special spirit that bonds people who are involved in achieving it," says Roger. "Somehow, things jell and fall together, and the project takes on a meaning of its own.

"The period of the early '60s was, in Quebec, a turning point in terms of social orientation, opening the province to newer trends. There was a lot of ferment and initiative in various fields, and road construction became part of a way to allow society to expand and become more mobile. In the currents of the time, it was an appropriate gesture to make."

The Trans-Canada around Montreal has since grown to be one of the busiest sections along the entire route, and it takes a special kind of driver to face the cut and thrust of its traffic every day. "You can't be afraid of the wheel," says Angel Catalan, a handsome, dark-haired young officer with the *Sûreté du Quebec's* highway patrol. "If you're scared of traffic, forget it. Go do something else."

Angel's beat includes Highway 40 just south of Montreal, eight lanes of constantly bobbing and weaving commuters and commercial traffic. It's not a place for the slow of reflex or the fragile of nerve. "You have to be able to maneuver yourself through the gridlock," says Angel, his police cruiser slipping in and around traffic like a speedy winger skating for open ice. "We've had people that have broken down in the gridlock and abandoned their cars because they couldn't take the pressure. The officer would get there, and they would literally tell us to tow the car away: 'I've had a rough day; call me a taxi.'"

Policing that kind of traffic calls for a keen eye, an understanding ear and a firm hand. Angel doesn't hesitate when a speeder blows by his radar gun. An uncooperative motorist is asked if he wants to be arrested and have his car towed. If something doesn't seem right when he pulls a driver over, he'll dig a little deeper to find out if there's a reason. Cops like him learn to trust their instincts. "The Trans-Canada has so much of everything," he says. "Good people, bad people—there's everything there. I'd be a fool to think everybody's good, but when I stop people, I think people are good until they prove to me they're not."

Sometimes it's not so easy to tell who's who. One day, Angel was patrolling when he got a call about someone driving an electric wheelchair on the highway. He drove over and sure enough, there was a man in an

Angel Catalan patrols one of the busiest stretches of the Trans-Canada—Highway 40 just south of Montreal—with a fearless feel for the road, a firm hand, a careful regard for his fellow drivers and a sense of humour.[50]

electric wheelchair heading north, a bright orange flag snapping back and forth in the breeze. Angel stopped him. The man told him the salesman who sold him the wheelchair had told him it would take him all the way to Quebec City, and he was simply trying it out. Angel was skeptical. He went back to his cruiser to check the man out and soon learned there was a warrant for his arrest.

Meanwhile, passers-by were wondering why the police had driven up, lights blazing, to stop this nice old man in a wheelchair. "All of a sudden, I'm the bad guy," Angel says. "People are yelling obscenities at me, all kinds of things. We ended up towing his wheelchair. I ended up picking him up and putting him in my car, and away we went."

The construction of the Trans-Canada Highway was a powerful source of social change everywhere, but nowhere was the impact of the road more widespread and powerful than in Newfoundland. When Newfoundland joined Confederation in 1949, its roads weren't that much different than they had been in 1914. The generation that fought the Second World War was using the same paths marched on by those who fought the First. There were a few paved roads, the longest being from St. John's around Conception Bay to Harbour Grace, but the vast majority of the island's 1,300 communities were tied together only by narrow gravel roads that were impassable in the heavy snowfall of a Newfoundland winter. For six months of the year, Newfoundlanders were cut off from one another, their towns and outports accessible only by braving the blustery North Atlantic.

Building highways on the Rock wasn't much easier than building them through the Shield or Rogers Pass. Newfoundland had the same old enemies in abundance: lakes, rivers, muskeg and great fists of gnarled rock.

This 1952 photo from near Tompkins, Newfoundland, gives a good view of the old adversaries highway crews faced all over the country: heavy bush and heavy rock.[51]

The muskeg was often 15 metres (50 feet) deep, deep enough to swallow earthmovers and far too deep to excavate, as had been done in the Shield. Crews simply tipped load after uncounted load of rock into the swampy goo to fill and stabilize it. It took thousands of tons of crushed rock to make the muskeg stable enough to build on. Fortunately, fill wasn't hard to find. They call it the Rock for a reason, and engineers had to blast out virtually the entire 834-kilometre (518-mile) route, sometimes to a depth of nine metres (30 feet). Nor were they simply widening and improving an earlier road. Much of the Trans-Canada went through land that was entirely untouched.

Still, the work got done. Building the Trans-Canada Highway, which wasn't complete through the province until 1965, became the centrepiece of an extensive road-building program. Between 1949 and 1964, the province built 3,500 kilometres (2,100 miles) of new road and rebuilt another 4,025 kilometres (2,500 miles). A total of 225 bridges were constructed.

Percy Barrett is now Newfoundland's minister in charge of highways, but in 1965 he was a teenager visiting the province's capital, about to witness life on the Rock change utterly. "I remember the day that the Trans-Canada was opened," he says. "I was there as a very young teenager, and the motorcade that left St. John's was three kilometres (two miles) long. It was a great celebration day in Newfoundland."

With good reason. When Barrett grew up on Woody Island in Placentia Bay on Newfoundland's rugged southeast coast, a trip to St. John's took all day. Now, it was an easy two-and-a-half hour drive. Doctors and nurses could get out to visit the sick, and the sick could get to hospitals. Road-building paved the way for electricity and telephones. Social services were improved. The one- and two-room schoolhouses that had characterized the outports for generations slowly disappeared in favour of centralized, larger, better-equipped high schools, resulting in an almost immediate improvement in education. In 1955 a student in a village one-room school had a one in 700 chance of graduating from Grade 11. By 1964 Newfoundland's government of the day bragged that children from such communities were graduating from Grade 11 at the same rate as children from St. John's or Montreal. One measure of the importance of the new highway to Newfoundlanders is that they are the only people in the country who habitually refer to the Trans-Canada Highway by its name rather than its number.

The Rock had to wait longer than anywhere else for the Trans-Canada Highway, but when it was finished, says Jim Case, Newfoundlanders took to it like no other Canadians.[52]

"It wasn't only the fact that people could commute back and forth and that we improved our utilities," says Barrett. "The Trans-Canada Highway also changed the social structure of Newfoundland. I grew up on an island in Placentia Bay, and the only people I knew were the other people on the island. And all of a sudden, I was able to visit people in other areas of the province, and it was just fantastic." The Trans-Canada Highway gave Newfoundlanders a whole new world—their own province.

Jim Case was seven years old in 1965 when the asphalt on the last stretch of the Trans-Canada was laid. For years his family had been listening to Premier Joey Smallwood's mantra of "Finish the Drive in '65." Now, here it was. Jim's father celebrated by going out and buying his first new car, a Chevy Bel Air—"four doors, a gorgeous big car," recalls Jim. And the Cases hit the road, anxious to have a look at a Newfoundland they'd never seen. "Newfoundland was your oyster," Jim says. "Boom—get on the road and go."

And they went. Every summer for nearly a decade, the Cases would hop in that blue Chevy, load up the tent trailer, and see a part of Newfoundland they'd never seen before. Islanders had to readjust their whole way of thinking. Eight kilometres (five miles) between towns that used to take all afternoon to walk could now be driven in a few minutes. Crossing the island, which previously could only be done by rail, could now be done anytime by anyone. "Everything changed after the highway came through," Jim says, still in awe at the wonder of being able to move freely, quickly and safely. "People had to adjust mentally to the fact that you could actually take a car. There was the blue Chevy, hands on the wheel, let's go. It was a hugely unifying event, it—really was. It was limitless. It was just open up the roadmap—boom."

CHAPTER 6

AFTER A COUPLE OF DAYS ON THE ROAD, THE CULVERS SLIPPED INTO A TRAVelling groove. The kilometres dropped by, 65 (40 miles) of them every hour. Dennis and Eleanor alternated between turns at the wheel and naps on the rear bench. The two switched driving shifts without stopping the bus. Since the gas pedal was always flat to the floor, it was a simple matter for a new foot to take over from the old one, leaving the retiring driver to slip out to the left in the space between the driver's seat and the door. Meanwhile, the older children rotated through their co-pilot shifts in the passenger's seat. Co-pilots were in charge of knowing where they were on the map, how far it was to the next stop, the location of the next diesel station, and keeping the driver fuelled with tea and almonds and entertained with conversation. The co-pilot's chair was eagerly anticipated. In a family of nine children, time alone with a parent was a rare treat.

The back of the bus was a busy place. In the days before mandatory seat belts, the kids weren't strapped down and were able to wander freely from seat to seat. In 1963 videos, music tapes and even radios were also in

the future, and entertainment on the road consisted of card games, a large stack of Classic Comics and time-honoured highway amusements such as trying to get passing vehicles to wave. Sometimes, everyone was peaceful, talking gently, playing solitaire or flipping through the brightly illustrated pages of *Moby Dick*. Sometimes, the kids got pretty raucous, not always with happy results. On one particularly hot day outside Ottawa, someone kicked over one of the latrine buckets. But if there were any disagreements among the children, the bus offered plenty of room to simply separate the combatants and restore peace. At night, Eleanor's curtains allowed lights to be kept on in the back without blinding the driver. The family slept in the big reclining seats or on the floor between them, padded with plenty of blankets and pillows.

The Culvers' heavily loaded bus was almost the slowest thing on the road. The only vehicle the Culvers managed to pass in the entire trip was a farm tractor pulling a wagon. But traffic was slower in those days, and the bus wasn't a hazard. And Dennis and Eleanor never hesitated to pull over and wave a faster driver by. Hills, however, could be a problem. One particularly steep incline in New Brunswick forced Dennis to leave the kids by the side of the road and drive up without them. Everyone followed behind on foot. And there were a couple mechanical problems: a broken fan, a dropped ground wire. Everything was readily fixed from Dennis' box of tools and parts. Nothing interfered with the orderly procession of the schedule.

It didn't take the Culvers long to meld into a finely honed travelling machine. Everyone knew their job and the miles and the meals slipped smoothly by.[53]

Once they found the rhythm of the road, the Culvers settled comfortably into life on the Trans-Canada. In fact, they were thriving on it. But every road creates two kinds of people: those travelling on it and those living beside it. Those in the second group quickly realized that they didn't have to drive the Trans-Canada for it to profoundly change their lives. The location of the Trans-Canada right-of-way was to become perhaps the single largest factor in the future of the communities beside it. For some, it became the road to opportunity. They knew the new highway was going to be a busy place. People in the endless stream of cars cruising by needed places to eat and stretch their legs, sometimes a place to stay overnight or even linger a bit. Like the Culvers, they thrived. For others, the highway siphoned away everything their community once had. And for some, the Trans-Canada became both. The highway gave, and the highway took away.

In 1961 engineers plotting the route of the Trans-Canada through the Fraser Valley in British Columbia ran into a small hitch in the town of Spences Bridge, 145 kilometres (90 miles) north of Hope. The old highway ran right through the middle of town, and there was no room for the Trans-Canada's 30-metre (100-foot) right-of-way. But going outside of town meant running right through the Nlaka' Pamux reserve. Negotiations ensued, which resulted in the band getting a small piece of land alongside the highway in compensation. Band members Joyce and Forest Walkem looked at the land, looked at the beautiful scenery around it, thought about the traffic soon to be running by it and decided that all those travellers would need a place to gas up, have a meal and maybe call it a day.

It may not sound like a bold and innovative idea, but it was. Businesses on reserves were almost always owned by band councils, not by individual band members. Joyce and Forest wanted to change tradition. They wanted to own their own business, not just manage it on the band's behalf. Their plan to run things themselves would make them among the first of a new generation of native businesspeople, and the band council was willing to let them give it a try. It passed a special resolution ensuring Joyce and Forest's tenure on the land so they could get bank financing. The banks weren't the main problem, however. The biggest doubters were the federal Indian Affairs bureaucrats. "It was a massive learning experience for Indian Affairs," says Joyce's son David, who was about six at the time. "I saw some of the letters from the Indian Agent at the time that were saying, 'Why don't you just build a campsite or a fruit stand? You know—something you can manage.' They didn't believe an Indian individual could do these things."

Joyce felt plenty of skepticism from people in Spences Bridge, too. Nobody wished them luck. People believed they'd last six months. "People were curious to see what a native family could do," she says.

She and Forest set out to show them. Their people had been successful traders for generations, establishing trade routes up and down the nearby valleys long before Europeans arrived. Many prospectors heading up to the Cariboo gold fields did so on horses and mules they bought from Joyce's family. So without a nickel from Indian Affairs or the band, the Walkems built The Sportsman, a motel, service station and 37-seat restaurant. It was complete with amenities like a playground, swimming pool and air-conditioned rooms—much appreciated by travellers coming in from the 38°C (100°F) summer heat.

The Sportsman prospered. Hunters loved the local herds of deer and bighorn sheep, some of which yielded record trophy heads. Fishermen flocked to the nearby Thompson River to hit the big runs of spring

The Sportsman Motel, shown in this postcard, was more than just a business for the Walkem family. It was an education and a window on the world—and a statement about what a native family could accomplish, given the opportunity.[54]

salmon and steelhead. Both groups snapped up the gear that Joyce and Forest were happy to sell them.

Forest looked after the guests who needed a guide. Uncles and cousins changed tires and pumped gas. In the restaurant, Joyce served meals cooked from scratch. She baked her own buns and pies and boiled her own soup stocks. Even her vegetables came from a big garden the family tended at the back of the hotel. Flowerbeds around the buildings were carefully maintained. Lawns were watered and mowed. Pavement was swept free of dust.

Fishing was good in the Thompson River, as proved by the good-sized salmon that Forest Walkem is showing off in this picture.[55]

"We were proud of what we did," says Joyce. "I'd never been in business before. I'd worked for other people, but I learned quickly. When I went into the restaurant, I had the thought that I was going to serve meals the way I wanted them served to me. And I think that's why I was successful. People appreciate it. I had people coming from all over just to have a meal. And that makes you feel good."

For a while, The Sportsman was the biggest employer in Spences Bridge. Joyce and her family met people from all over the world. But by the late 1970s, things were starting to slip. One factor was that the game in the hills and the fishing in the rivers weren't as plentiful any more. But the biggest change was in the way people travelled. The Trans-Canada got smoother, the cars got faster and more comfortable. Driving was getting easier and easier, and people were doing it for longer and longer stints. A four-hour leg from Vancouver with a stopover in Spences Bridge used to be the normal route. Now they were heading straight through. "We had six gas stations in Spences Bridge, and we all made a living," Joyce recalls. "It was a gas-up spot, an eating place or a place to sleep in the motel. And then it changed. People changed their mode of travel. Instead of getting up and leaving in the morning and making it to a stop-off place, they would just carry on through."

Joyce has no rancor or regret. Just the same matter-of-fact, hard-headed perception that allowed her to recognize the opportunity the highway offered in the first place. "People got in too much of a hurry. There was no such thing as getting to your destination in a relaxing way. It was running from A to B."

In 1981 the high-speed Coquihalla Highway through central British Columbia sucked traffic from the more meandering Trans-Canada, slowing business at Spences Bridge even more. Finally, in 1982, the Walkems left The Sportsman. It now sits abandoned by the side of the highway, weeds growing in the swimming pool, dust covering the restaurant tables that Joyce had kept so insistently polished. But David, who followed in his father's footsteps to become chief of the band, is grateful for what The Sportsman and the Trans-Canada gave him.

Joyce Walkem accepts the changes that eventually caused The Sportsman to close, but still remembers the days when travel was a bit more leisurely. Her son David is grateful to the Trans-Canada for providing both a living, and a life.[56]

"The Trans-Canada Highway offered my parents an opportunity to earn their own living and be their own bosses and raise a family. And it's done us very well that way. I feel very privileged. We have never been on welfare; my family has always worked hard. It has instilled in our family the need to work hard for a living. And the highway's provided us with a very good living. It helped give me opportunities to deal with people, deal with the public, deal with business. It helped raise me."

Burt Brown, back at his service station on the English River, would have recognized the pattern. Burt had shuttered the station for the duration of the Second World War, but when he returned to his idyllic, lakeside section of the Canadian Shield after the fighting was over, he had big plans. Ever since that first quiet winter in 1935, traffic had been steadily picking up along his stretch of the Trans-Canada. Even before the war, he'd noticed that most of the people driving through were there for the fishing and the hunting. It was time to act on the plan that had been in back of his mind all along: a tourist camp, offering guide services, comfortable cabins and boats. As with the Walkems, Burt's timing was perfect. The road was still rough, but wartime gas rationing had created a pent-up demand for travel, and people were on the move despite the bumps and potholes. There was money to spend and the time and inclination to spend it. Brown's Service Station changed its name to Brown's Tourist Camp for the 1950 season, and before long, Burt added a lodge and a restaurant and had 25 people on the payroll.

The camp was a busy place. Brown's could accommodate almost 100 people, and in peak season it was nearly always packed. Americans from Wisconsin and Iowa flocked over the border to the unspoiled Shield country, where Burt could line them up with a fishing guide who would take them to a lake where theirs was the only boat. Kids swam off the 32-metre (100-foot) dock, and guests swapped fish stories in the lodge. Moose and bear hunters kept Burt busy long into the fall. "The most enjoyable part was catering to people that really were enthused about it," he says. "I would take a party into a lake that I had the only boat on, and nobody else would see it. When they were fishing, they'd often see moose come down to the water. Then they'd go berry-picking. And they'd appreciate going in there, and they'd just rave about it for ages. They'd return the next year and want to do the same thing again. I didn't spend ten cents for advertising all the time I was in business."

Eventually things changed, just as they had for the Walkems. Maybe people got to be in too much of a hurry. Maybe the cars got too fast and comfortable. Maybe people just began to want something more than a rustic cabin and a shore lunch. But Burt thinks that getting around became too easy. A couple hours drive to a fishing camp by the side of the highway wasn't that big a deal any more.

"Travel was more of an adventure in the early days," he says. "In the old days you couldn't depend on getting to your destination when you wanted to. Now, it's all taken for granted. The people jump in the car, and they'll be in Regina tonight and Edmonton the next night. It's all laid out." Whatever the changes were, they weren't good for business. By the time Burt sold out in 1967, Brown's was a shadow of what it once had been.

Smoother roads, better cars, longer drives—it's been a triple whammy powerful enough to affect much more than individual businesses. The same pattern plays out on a much larger scale. The prairies are dotted with towns and villages spaced at the distance a farmer used to be able to drive a team of horses in a day or how far a steam locomotive could go before needing fuel and water. The new highway made those old measures of distance irrelevant. The communities based on them, now bypassed by the safe, fast Trans-Canada, struggle to escape the same fate.

Dennis Edwards' grandfather came to the Saskatchewan prairie in the 1890s to work as a ranch hand and blacksmith on one of the big cattle operations of the time. Killing winters eventually drove the cattle baron he worked for out of business, and A.W. Edwards drifted north to Broadview,

outside Regina. There he started selling farm equipment, becoming a dealer for what was then the Massey company. Dennis' father kept the business going through the Depression, and after the Second World War his uncle returned from overseas to help out. Dennis and his brother ran a gas station by the highway for a while but eventually sold that to return to the family roots. The three generations of Edwards' that have run the dealership, as well as the changing fortunes of the company, are reflected on its walls, where A.W. Edwards' old Massey-Harris posters share space with the latest Massey-Ferguson dealer's calendar. The business is still run out of the same sturdy building that old A.W. erected. But Dennis figures his generation will be the last.

The original Edwards building, constructed in 1896, became the heart of what grew into a century-long family business serving the farmers around Broadview, Saskatchewan. That dynasty, however, is in danger.[57]

The interior of the Edwards dealership mixes décor from the entire long history of the dealership. Dennis and Ally Edwards' business is changing, however, as small-town dealerships move away from selling big-ticket machinery to providing service and parts.[58]

"The heritage here that my brother and I have carried forward is absolutely tremendous, but I don't think it's going to go any further," he says, his businesslike phone manner giving way to a tone of gentle regret. "Our families are up and grown away, and I can't foresee in the next ten to fifteen years that there's going to be a single implement dealer in small-town Saskatchewan."

The reasons are the stuff of a hundred newspaper stories, but Dennis and his family haven't had to read them. They've watched the process first-hand. In A.W. Edwards' day, the land around Broadview in the Pipestone Valley was homesteaded in quarter section lots. Every 60 hectares (150 acres) there was another farm, and every farm needed a cream separator, a

binder, a washing machine, a plow. The nearest town—often the only town it was possible to reach—was Broadview. As well, the CPR had 200 employees in town to maintain and fuel its steam locomotives. These days the average farm in Saskatchewan is about 525 hectares (1,300 acres). When the railway changed over to diesel locomotives, 150 jobs left Broadview almost overnight. The town's population had slipped from a peak of about 1,200 to a stable 700. But one of the biggest challenges in Broadview's struggle to find a new role has been the Trans-Canada Highway.

"The Trans-Canada Highway to Broadview made the bigger cities more accessible to our trading public," Dennis says. "A lot of our people make the trip into Regina. The Trans-Canada is taking a lot of shoppers out of the community; therefore, the volume of trade is not as great as it used to be. We had to expand our trading area from about 35 kilometres (20 miles) around Broadview to 130 or 135 kilometres (80 or 85 miles) away. We're dealing with the same number of people that we used to, but to maintain the volume that's required, you're going 130 kilometres (80 miles) away quite consistently."

As customers blow down the road like tumbleweeds, so do businesses. One Broadview street is lined with shuttered windows and empty buildings. Dennis recalls when the town had its own meat market. The local Bank of Commerce is gone. So are the other machinery dealerships. Imperial Oil and Federated Co-op have hauled away the bulk fuel tanks that used to serve the area.

In 1973 the Canadian Transportation Commission hired a sociologist to look at the effects of improved transportation on prairie communities. J.C. Stabler's first finding was that, yes, roads had certainly improved. In 1941 Alberta, Saskatchewan and Manitoba had less than 2,250 kilometres

(1,400 miles) of paved road among them. By 1968 they had nearly 29,000 (18,000 miles). The pace quickened during the 1960s, when more than half the hard-surfaced intercity prairie highways were paved and about a third of the grid roads were upgraded. Stabler then focussed his research on the Qu'Appelle Basin around Regina, trying to determine the effect of all that road-building. He found that in 1961 there had been 68 communities in the study area offering no more than basic services, such as a gas station, a school, a grocery store. Those communities had averaged between five and thirteen retail outlets. By 1970 there were 72 communities that could offer their residents no more than the basics. At the same time, the average number of stores in those 72 communities had shrunk to between three and nine. Stabler also looked at the different types of businesses in the towns. He found that business diversity grew in only nine communities during the study period, while it shrank in 38. In short, there were more and more small towns with less and less to offer.

The findings got even more discouraging. Stabler found that medium-sized communities were hit as hard as the smallest ones. When people from tiny towns go shopping, they don't just head to the next biggest community. They head all the way into Regina. Stabler even worked out a mathematical formula to determine the likelihood of someone staying at home to shop versus heading down the highway. "Attraction of a central place is directly related to its size and inversely related to the time expended on a trip to it," he wrote. "Since time spent in preparation for a shopping trip and in finding a parking space is invariant with distance, equal improvement in access to all centres would strengthen the attraction of larger, more distant places relative to closer, smaller ones. If access to the larger centre is improved relative to that of smaller places, its attraction is further enhanced."

When Shirley Gwilliam, Summerberry's last postmistress, finally closed her wicket for the last time, she closed down her town, too.[59]

Stabler's findings wouldn't have been news to Shirley Gwilliam. She knows all about it. In 1994 she became one of the last holdouts to leave Summerberry, Saskatchewan, after living there for 39 years. The buildings still stand. The school has been turned into a museum, old-fashioned student desks still sitting in rows. But the people are gone, and when she returns it's to a town of boarded-up windows, the only voices those of leaves rustling in the prairie breeze.

"When we moved here, the grocery stores were fully stocked with everything you could want," Shirley says. "So was the hardware. If you needed gas, you needed repairs, you needed any appliance, you could get it. My husband and I loved Summerberry. We liked the small towns where

It may have been—literally—only a wide spot in the road, but Summerberry, Saskatchewan was home to hundreds over the years. Now, it lies empty along the Trans-Canada.[60]

Summerberry was once full of scenes like this, with sports days in summer, street hockey in winter and a small school full of bright, shining faces.[61, 62]

you could get around, know your neighbours, know where you were going and how to get there and how long it's going to take you."

Shirley remembers how Summerberry's Christmas concerts drew people from all over. Summer sports days would bring out a dozen local ball teams. And in the winter, people curled and skated. Now, she ticks off her town's slow decline: the school closing in '66; the curling rink and hardware store gone in '69. One store gone in '70, the other in '74. The church sold and moved in '84. "It's very sad to see your church going down the road," she says. "Where are you going to go?"

And then in 1988 the *coup de grace*—the tearing down and burning of the three grain elevators. "To see all that lumber go to waste," she says as she shakes her head, prairie frugality masking her sorrow. "Just up in smoke."

Shirley was Summerberry's postmistress, and when she gave that up in 1993 and moved to nearby Grenfell, the last little bit of the town died with it.

"We moved away and took Summerberry with us," says Shirley, at last permitting herself a ghostly smile. "My attachment to Summerberry is at the cemetery. My husband's buried there, I've got a granddaughter buried there, and I've got a great-grandson buried there. Otherwise, I haven't got much attachment. It's just the cemetery now."

Prairie communities haven't been the only ones to feel pressure from the Trans-Canada Highway. Mulgrave, Nova Scotia, used to be a busy little transportation hub. Anyone heading to Cape Breton Island from the mainland had to drive through Mulgrave, where a train ferry took people across the Strait of Canso.

A directory of Nova Scotia communities once described it as "one of the most important railroad centres in the Maritime Provinces." Mulgrave boasted stores, hotels, a lobster factory and four churches. But it all

Mulgrave's car ferry was an important part of the ferry service on which the busy little town of Mulgrave, Nova Scotia, once depended.[63]

depended on the railway ferry, which employed two-thirds of the town's workers. When plans were laid for a permanent bridge to Cape Breton, local residents felt a chill fall over their future.

In 1951 Mulgrave mayor Leonard O'Neill gave eloquent expression to that chill in a pleading brief he wrote to the provincial government. "After 50 years of stable growth, the community of Mulgrave faces disaster. The haunting fear of insecurity lies pregnant on the thresholds of her homes. The stability of family life is threatened; and the carefully nurtured traditions from which a lively community spirit has been fostered are in danger of fading into oblivion."

O'Neill wanted the provincial government to think hard about the effect that the Canso Causeway would have on his town, but it was to no avail. Construction started in the autumn of 1952, and three years and $20 million later, 100 pipers marched across the causeway to celebrate its opening on August 13, 1955. Crowds cheered the new link, but Lillian Williams, who has lived in Mulgrave all her 104 years, wasn't among them.

"We lost everything when the causeway went through," she says.

Her memories are of the idyllic small town described in O'Neill's letter: lots of friends with whom to skate on frozen ponds or roam over the hills; chugging up and down the strait in little motorboats, lobsters for the catching; watching the moon rise over the open water; ferry rides along the coast. When constructions workers started blasting for the causeway, it shook every home in Mulgrave. "Oh, they were terrible blasts," Lillian says. "One night I had company here, and when the blast came, you'd think there was something come through the side of the house. I think every cellar in Mulgrave cracked."

As the daughter of a man who used to work on the old train ferry, and as someone who has watched the slow decline of the only home she's ever known, there's a hard, unforgiving note in her voice when she talks about the Canso Causeway. "That was the death blow to Mulgrave," she says. "Overnight, we were left with nothing and have got nothing since. The politicians have forgotten us down here altogether."

The same debate began all over again a couple generations later with the Confederation Bridge linking Prince Edward Island with the New Brunswick mainland. Some form of fixed link was an old idea in Canada's smallest province. A proposal for a tunnel under the Northumberland Strait dates back to 1885, and the federal government

Lillian Williams, 104, still remembers the way things used to be in Mulgrave before the Canso Causeway—and she liked it better before.[64]

first planned a combined causeway, bridge and tunnel in 1965, plans that were later scrapped in favour of an enhanced ferry service that provided more jobs. Finally, in 1987, Ottawa put the fixed link project out for public tender, and the controversy began in earnest. What about the hundreds of ferry jobs that would be lost? What about the environmental impact? What about the impact of increased traffic and tourism on the island way of life? And when it became clear that the project was going to be a bridge, not a tunnel, fears only increased. A bridge would create ice jams and damage the local fishery, people worried. It wouldn't even be safe to drive in the high winds that howl down the strait. The opposition was loud and large. In a 1988 plebiscite, 40 percent of islanders voted against the fixed link.

The Canso Causeway, seen here under construction, was completed in 1955 and linked Cape Breton Island with the mainland, forever changing lives on both sides of the bridge.[65]

Nevertheless, it was clear that the bridge project was going to proceed, and resentment among its opponents was bitter. In 1993, in a critical book entitled *Crossing That Bridge*, journalist Lorraine Begley wrote:

> About a quarter century ago . . . a decision was made by the dominant elite that Prince Edward Island should abandon emphasis on its traditional resource-based economy of farming and fishing and concentrate instead on the service industry—tourism. Part of the process of 'selling' Prince Edward Island to a largely urban market in central Canada and the northeastern United States was to 'kidnap' the structure of ideas and cultural forms by which Prince Edward Islanders think of themselves. . . .
>
> Articulators of the 'Island Way of Life,' in trying to build an oppositional movement using the semantics of the Department of Tourism, have become stuck fast in the quicksand of those semantics. As a result, proponents of the 'Island Way of Life' were seen as 'backward,' while pro-bridge boosters were allowed to cast themselves as the voice of progress. . . . The proponents of the bridge managed to marginalize an opposition expressing itself in the language of community, home and the 'Island Way of Life' as nostalgic echoes of the traditionalism and quaintness to which, paradoxically, their fixed crossing will improve market access.

A private consortium, Strait Crossing Inc., eventually won the contract for the 13-kilometre (eight-mile) long bridge. Unique on the Trans-Canada, it would be a toll bridge, with Straight Crossing owning and oper-

ating it for 35 years after its construction. Drivers would pay nothing to get to Prince Edward Island, but leaving would cost $37.50.

The Confederation Bridge, completed in 1997, was the controversial culmination of more than three decades of debate on linking Prince Edward Island with the Canadian mainland.[66]

Construction of the fixed link began in 1994. At its peak 2,500 workers toiled at the project. Before they were through, they had poured nearly a half-million cubic yards of concrete braced with 50,000 tonnes of steel. Confederation Bridge opened in the spring of 1997 with a three-day festival that included music, displays and races across the bridge. On May 31, at 5:15 P.M., the first vehicles lined up to pay the toll.

Jamie Fox is a police officer on the island end of the bridge, chief of police for the community of Borden–Carlton. The bridge has had the anticipated effect, he observes.

Jamie Fox, who built a gas station at one end of Confederation Bridge, believes the bridge is an inevitable result of people demanding to be able to move quickly and easily. It's best to adapt to that, he says.[67]

"I think the bridge actually opened up the island. It makes it more accessible now in any weather, any time of year, whether it be day or night. And with that, it makes people move more. They can come faster, and go back whenever they want. You see a lot more people coming over for day-trips to golf or to go to the beaches. It has opened up the island for economic growth, it's opened up the island for tourism and it's provided the people with more of a connection to the country. We're not as isolated as we were."

Are mobility and connection good things? Fox thinks they are. In fact, he's taken advantage of the new restlessness and has built a prosperous gas station right at the foot of the bridge.

"People want to move quickly between provinces, from one place to another, and the Trans-Canada's adapting to that. What I saw was an opportunity to build with that change."

Adapting to change is the only way small towns along the Trans-Canada will survive. Dennis Edwards says the dealership still earns a decent income, although in the future it will probably shift more and more to selling parts and repairs instead of big-ticket machinery. And local pride, part of what gives small-towners the will to survive, dies hard. When Dennis and his brother celebrated the family's 100th year in business, 700 people crowded the street to offer congratulations and munch hot dogs.

Nevertheless, the small-town landscape alongside the Trans-Canada Highway feels increasingly emptied. Abandoned towns, abandoned farmsteads, abandoned machinery rusting by the road emanate a powerful sense of deserted hopes and unresolved mystery. Who were these people? What happened to them? The seemingly open land and sky in fact conceals much, hiding in plain sight the story of the vanished, unknown people

Strange things happen in Robert Kroetsch's novels, but no stranger, for him, than the ghost stories he sees on every drive along the Trans-Canada Highway.[68]

who once lived here. Those concealed mysteries are a wellspring of prairie writing. Poet and novelist Robert Kroetsch, who grew up in small-town Alberta, has drunk from that well his entire literary life. "People tell me sometimes there's nothing to look at between Winnipeg and Calgary, and that just infuriates me because every two miles [three kilometres] are different for me on that highway," he says. "It isn't the Rocky Mountains or the Precambrian Shield; it's a very subtle change of human habitation. You know—history that came and went, small towns that came and went in less than a hundred years."

Strange things happen in his books, such as *The Studhorse Man* or *What the Crow Said.* But in a way, Kroetsch says he's only reflecting what has actually happened to his boyhood landscape.

> The highway has turned the prairies into a ghost story because very few urban centres have emerged. There are many of these abandoned but remembered small towns. We have a trace. We have photographs of hockey teams, we have old people telling wonderful stories, we have recollections of the old grain elevators which were once the markers of the prairie. But they have become a ghostly presence. And as you drive along the Trans-Canada, you see these incredibly attractive graveyards that seem to be maintained by nobody. One little town I see as I drive by haunts me as one of those places that has become a ghost. It's still visible there, and yet it's ghostly. One of the things the highway has done has been to create a sense of ghostliness, a presence of what is there but not there, which is what a ghost is all about. So I like that.

A grain elevator and a branch line railway track: two vanishing symbols of prairie life, replaced and turned into ghosts by the Trans-Canada Highway.[69]

One time, when I was driving west, I stopped in Rogers Pass. I went in to see if they had a room, and the clerk said there was one room left. I was filling out a form and a woman came in with a baby that was crying and I said 'Give her the room, I feel like driving.' So I drove farther west, and after I passed Golden, all of a sudden I became sleepy. So I found this little place by the road. I went in and there were two very old people running it, and it was almost as if they'd been waiting for me. They gave me a room, but a couple hours later I woke up again, wired the way you sometimes are when you're driving. I left some money on the dresser and I drove on.

"On the way back, I decided to stop there. But I couldn't find it. It was as if the place had vanished or I'd imagined it. But it was a real place, I did stop there. It's more real to me than any other hotel I stayed in along the highway, but I can't find it. And that's the story of the Trans-Canada Highway for me."

CHAPTER 7

EVENTUALLY, EVEN THE LONGEST ROAD COMES TO AN END. THE FIFTH DAY OF their cross-country journey found the Culvers cruising through the green landscape of Nova Scotia, closer and closer to the home of Eleanor's sister. Even though it was the early hours of the morning and the bus had been on the highway all night, most of the family was too excited to sleep. The New Brunswick border had been reached at the appointed hour, and for the first time in five days, Dennis was feeling no anxiety about the schedule. He was at the wheel, driving comfortably, not pushing the bus too hard. They were going to make it.

As dawn approached, the Culver's bus rolled into Pictou, Nova Scotia, and clattered up the hill toward the home of Eleanor's sister Noni. They pulled into the driveway at 6:00 A.M., two hours ahead of schedule.

The triumphant arrival scene, however, was anticlimactic. Noni wasn't home. Not sharing Dennis' faith in planning, she was still on her way back from the family's summer cottage on Northumberland Strait. The Culvers shrugged, walked back to the bus, curled up in the reclining seats and had

a nap while they waited. Finally, Noni appeared, and her surprise to find that her west coast relatives had beaten her home was highly gratifying to Dennis. "Her head appeared as she walked up the hill on the side street at about 8:15," he recalls. "The look of shocked incredulity as she saw our bus sitting in front of her home is a memory which still brings much pleasure to me."

The Culvers' trip was over. But it was only the first of many marathon journeys the family was to take in the old Mercedes bus. There was the trip home, of course, a more leisurely two-week drive at the end of the summer with a cousin from the east coming back with them. A few years later, there was a drive out to Montreal for Expo 67. And there were many cruises to favourite cabins on British Columbia's Quesnel Lake. That first trip, however, is remembered with special fondness. The tracks it left on all eleven members of the family have lingered. "The favourite part of the trip for me wasn't necessarily the scenery or the highway or the place where we were going," recalls Bruce Culver. "It was just being with the family, playing games in the car and just hanging out. It was an adventure. That was the best part—just hanging out with the family."

Travelling the Trans-Canada brought the Culvers closer and taught them to how to work together. Everyone played a role, from the planning right through to the moment they rolled up to their destination. Dennis tells a story from one of their Quesnel trips that sums up the mark the Trans-Canada left on his family. The Culvers were staying in a rented cabin near the lake when the resort owner's daughter came to tell them that a heavy wind was blowing up and that their boat, tied up at the wharf, was in danger. "I said 'Come on, kids,'" says Dennis. "Everybody jumped to their feet. The youngsters and I ran down and waded into the water. Somebody untied the rope, and this 115-kilogram (250-pound) boat was whisked up the bank and laid down about 12 metres (40 feet) in from the water. When we left to go back and have dinner, the old caretaker turned to me and said, 'Sir, you've got some power there.' And I think that says it all. We work together in any kind of a joint venture."

But bonds formed on the road aren't restricted to family. Or perhaps it's more accurate to say that the road creates its own family. "Everybody here I consider my family," says Ed Schmitt, gesturing out toward the midway. "There's people here that I call uncle or aunt. There's one lady here that I used to call my mom."

Sometimes that means looking after each other. Ed's girlfriend, Debbie, has earned the nickname Mother Hen for the watchful eye she keeps on the young girls that join the midway family. "It gives them somebody to talk to if they've got problems. I keep an eye on them so they don't do something stupid and the guys don't take advantage of them. Usually I go

over and say, 'Hey guys, back off. You should know better.' I leave it at that. If it continues, I say something different."

People on the road together simply have to get to know each other, says Ed. Cut off from their former homes, set apart form the community they're visiting, fellow travellers are thrown back on one another. They are forced to learn to count on their companions. "You've got to do this," says Ed. "Otherwise, you can't work together."

Hockey teams understand that, concluded Bob Ridley. Travelling together from one hostile arena to another, while learning how to savour victory or swallow defeat, is the fastest way create the bond that successful teams need. "A lot of these teams like to get out on the road early in the season just to do some team bonding and bring the players together," he says. "Coaches find that they gel better as a team more quickly if they can get out on the road. Teams try to plan their season with a fairly lengthy road trip right off the bat. It's kind of ploy. All these teams' general managers try to get the team going early and coming out of the gate running."

Perhaps the best way to learn about the need to bond with fellow travellers is to try travelling alone. Being alone on the road far from home and late at night is about as lonely a place as there is. Bonita Garret learned all about that kind of loneliness. After her Trans-Canada flight from her abusive husband, she eventually remarried to a man who was a long-haul trucker. Bonita has always enjoyed driving, so she learned to operate a big rig herself. Then as now, a female trucker on the road is a rarity, and Bonita could always find hours of conversation on the CB radio with other drivers who were grateful to hear a woman's voice. She calls that time a wonderful adventure, but her memories are marked by the isolation of a trucker's life.

"There is a reason there aren't a lot of women out there," she says. "The days are long. You're by yourself. You shower when you stop for fuel. There aren't a lot of people to see and interact with unless it's on the CB, and usually you're going one way and they're going the other."

One night she pulled into a truck-stop parking lot for the night and a man came around, knocked on her door and asked her if she required "service." When she said she just wanted a night's sleep, the man told her she had parked in a section of the lot reserved for truckers looking for a visit from a prostitute. An attendant came around every morning at 5 A.M. and swept up the used condoms.

"Long-haul trucking was an awful lot harder than I'd anticipated," she says. "It was a lot more lonesome than I'd expected. There's an entirely different subculture out there, and it's lonesome. It's not the way I was raised."

The isolation and vulnerability of travellers sometimes leads them to look out for one another even when they're not travelling together. Sometimes, the simple fact of being on the road is connection enough. Time after time, Allan and Donna Kelly found people watching out for them and giving them a hand when something went wrong. One day, as the couple was clip-clopping into Thunder Bay, Allan had an accident with the wagon and ended up in the ditch, the rig's two front wheels snapped right off. Before long, a truck pulled over that had a welding torch in the back. A couple in a motorhome stopped and offered the Kellys a shower and a hot meal. People brought hay for their horses. The next day the Kellys resumed their trek, the wagon repaired as good as new.

Truckers, too, looked out for the Kellys. The wagon only made about 35 kilometres (20 miles) a day, and the same drivers passed by them again and again, going back and forth along their regular routes. Eventually, the truckers started using their radios to let each other know where the Kellys were and how they were doing. And one afternoon the Kellys rounded a curve to find more than a dozen big rigs pulled over in a rest area. The drivers had barbecues going and hamburgers on the grill. They hosted a party for the Kellys right there by the side of the road. They'd even taken up a collection to help them on their way.

Something in the Kellys' trip seemed to touch people. "The miles we could go in a day usually depended upon how many times we were stopped by people," says Donna. Local newspapers wrote features on them. One woman invited them to her eight-year-old son's birthday party. A man pulled over and slipped Allan a twenty-dollar bill, saying "God be with you. I wish I could join you." Police officers on highway patrol invited them home for supper. One day, when they were rolling over a bridge in an Indian reserve, a group of band members paddled by on the river, beached their canoes and walked over with armloads of groceries. Allan joked, "You better be careful or we'll form a circle," and everyone laughed.

Allan and Donna even began their married life with a group of people they'd met on the road. Outside of Thunder Bay, a woman pulled over to talk to them. She'd heard about them, what their plans were and that they were engaged. Why not get married right here in Thunder Bay? she asked, and she talked the couple into it. Somebody lent Allan a suit and Donna a dress. A minister and church were found. The Kellys became husband and wife, celebrating with a tableload of sandwiches and ginger ale in a roomful of people they'd never met before. Donna still has her two wedding gifts: a beautiful serving plate and a kitchen container.

The Kellys had hit the Trans-Canada en route, they hoped, to a new life. Slowly, however, their destination grew less important as the road itself began to reveal that new life to them. In the closeness of their day-to-day experience together and in the contact and connection they made with stranger after stranger, they began to sense a new kind of arrival. They were finding a new life, all right. It just wasn't turning out to be the one they thought they were headed for.

Donna, Don and Allan Kelly formed a deep bond during their time together travelling the Trans-Canada. And again and again, they found other people looking out for them as well.[70]

Allan, Donna and Leroy the horse made it as far as Sudbury that first summer. As the days got colder and the couple's finances grew dimmer, they realized it was time to settle the rig for the winter and find jobs. They worked briefly at a racetrack, then at a ranch out of town. When spring came, plans were made to resume the journey. But before they threw the harness on old Leroy, Donna got a call from her brother Bob back in Montreal. Like his sister before him, he was dissatisfied with his life. He didn't know what he wanted, but he knew he had to make some changes and was thinking about moving to Toronto. Moving wasn't going to change anything, Donna told him. If you want something different, why not join us?

The Kellys had a good laugh when they picked up Bob at the Thunder Bay airport. Just as they had been at the start, Bob was dressed in full western regalia down to the big hunting knife, duster and Australian cowboy hat. Nevertheless, the three headed out toward the prairie. They made it through Winnipeg and as far as Portage la Prairie when they had to stop. Donna's horse had a sore foot. They nursed the horse for a week, but a vet told them that it wouldn't be able to continue. While they were deciding what to do, Donna went in for an appendix operation and found out she was pregnant. The three settled in for another winter, intending to resume the journey when the weather warmed up.

The next spring, however, with new baby Brent, travel didn't seem like such a good idea. The following spring found them short of money. So did the spring after that. And eventually the Kellys settled in. They bought a piece of land near East Braintree, Manitoba, started a ranch, and there they stayed. They hadn't realized it at first, but they had reached the end of a trip that became the defining act of their lives.

The highway eventually took the Kellys to the new life they were looking for. It wasn't where they thought it was going to be or the kind of life they were expecting, but the couple has no regrets.[71, 72]

"The trip brought us closer to Christ, for one thing," said Donna. "It brought us closer to each other, and it gave us a sense of what people are like when they're connected to you. Travelling the Trans-Canada Highway was all about meeting great people who gave us a part of their character as they gave us their support. That, and getting closer to the animals, knowing that they really do have a personality and that they're very intelligent."

Allan credits their time riding in the wagon with cementing their marriage and laying the foundation for their future lives together. "Donna and I became closer than ever, which proved to us we that had a future together," he says. Some days were kind of rough and we were struggling through, but I'm glad the way things worked out because we've got a great family and we're closer than ever. I think the trip helped us grow that closeness."

Bob found a new life, too. One day along the highway in Manitoba, Allan went into a gas station for some sandwiches and ended up in a long conversation with the owner. The wagoneers wound up staying at his place for three days, and when they were stalled in Portage la Prairie, he offered them all jobs for the winter. Bob got to know the man's daughter. A couple years later, they were married. The two have lived in Winnipeg ever since.

"It was a lifetime experience for me," says Bob. "I wouldn't get on horseback and covered wagon again. I think those days are over for me. But I certainly wouldn't swap the experiences we had and all the people we met."

Barb Mitchell, too, calls her summer of hitchhiking on the Trans-Canada a marker that delineated a turning point in her life. She had gone from high school to university without really noticing much difference. She was still walking from classroom to classroom, underlining passages in textbooks, meeting people who were doing much the same as she was and who were from the same kinds of families as she was. Now, she was getting near the end of her studies. Soon she would have to find her place in a world she felt she didn't know much about. That one summer of trusting her fate to the road and to whatever her upraised thumb brought her way gave her the confidence she needed. She met people who had played no role in her affluent, middle-class youth. Her first ride heading out of Vancouver was a poor single mother. Her second ride was a pair of Saskatchewan cowboys in an ancient Oldsmobile, who took a shine to her and her friend and tried to buy them a farewell drink. Her third ride was a trucker.

"I met a lot of people who were not nearly as well off as I was, who in many cases didn't have high school education let alone university," she says. "They weren't making a lot of money. And I could see that, to them, driving on the Trans-Canada Highway was just part of their daily routine. It was not adventurous or romantic for them at all. It was just a means to get from one place in Canada where they were working to another place in Canada where they needed to go to work.

"Through hitchhiking I learned a lot about my own independence. Hitchhiking that great distance and seeing my great country gave me something. When you're down and you're frightened and you feel like you'll never make it in this world, you can bring up something from the depths. You can bring a knowledge that you have done something dangerous and you got by it. You know, if you can meet these cowboys in Saskatchewan and handle them, then surely you can go to *Maclean's* magazine and handle the public relations guy."

The Trans-Canada taught a similar lesson to Colleen Deschamps. She had taken off down the highway hoping the simplicity and quiet of travelling and living in her car would point the way to God. Instead, she found

Today, Barb Mitchell credits hitchhiking the Trans-Canada Highway with introducing her to types of people she'd never encountered before, as well as her first lessons in self-reliance.[73]

Him in the people she met along the way. Colleen and her friend, Rachel, made it all the way to the eastern terminus of the highway, hitchhiking to St. John's, Newfoundland, to save the cost of the ferry when they realized they didn't have a place to stay. Undaunted, Colleen walked over to the nearest phone booth and started dialing numbers at random. A woman's voice answered the third call. "I told her, 'Hi. We're two people from B.C. living in our car. We've left the car in Scotia, we're hitchhiking across Newfoundland and we need a place to stay. Can you help us out?'" The woman on the other end was silent for a few moments, then told her of another family, the Van Dycks, who might welcome them. Colleen gave them a call, and Anna Van Dyck, somewhat to even her own surprise, agreed. Later that afternoon, she picked the girls up and took them home with her.

"It was kind of a surprise," Anna recalls. "We had to think about it and actually pray about it just to see if this was the right thing to do. We've taken in children as adopted children and foster children, and, you know, hospitality's a gift I think I've been given. It's a gift from the Lord. I just love people, and if I can help them in any way, that's what I'm there for."

Anna and Conrad Van Dyck took the girls in, fed them and let them shower and launder their clothes. "It was really a trusting environment," says Colleen. "There was no apprehension on their side. We found out they were Christians, and that was a big bond, too. We felt very directed to be there." Colleen and her friend stayed with the Van Dycks for days. The Van Dycks took the girls around the province to the tourist spots, introduced them to their friends, took them to church, picked partridge berries with them and shared their lives. Colleen and Rachel ended up referring to the Van Dycks as their honourary mom and dad, and the Van Dyck girls became honourary sisters. They kept in touch for years after Colleen and Rachel went back home, and the Van Dycks eventually came out to visit them.

Colleen and Rachel now refer to that trip as Turning Point '96.

"This trip was central to my whole life," Colleen says. "It was almost a graduation into adulthood, and it was a very spiritual journey as well. The Trans-Canada to us is very symbolic of being united with people who are all different but yet are one. We learned so much about the generosity of people and the genuine goodness, we think, of human nature."

Bhaktimarga Swami completed his journey from Victoria to St. John's after 214 days of walking and chanting. As he walked, the message he had turned to the Trans-Canada to teach him began to seep up through the soles of his sneakers. Along the way, he was dwarfed by the mountains, prairies and forests of Canada's outsized geography. He was buffeted by uncounted hundreds of semi-trailer trucks roaring by about a metre away. He was soaked by rain and whipped by wind. And more than once, he was forced to turn to the kindness of strangers for companionship and help. Life on the road was wearing away his pride, leaving humility in its place. Bhaktimarga embraced the lesson, forcing himself to walk on no matter how hot, wet or windy the conditions got, refusing to wait out eight hours of downpour in a coffee shop. He wanted to learn to submit to and accept nature's moods. He wanted to be able to receive compassion with the same spirit as he gave it. He wanted to defeat his pride utterly, and it was a struggle.

"I think the most humbling experience is dealing with the mind," he says. "When you're alone on the road for many hours, the Trans-Canada can be lonely. And you have to cope with yourself, with the thoughts in your mind. And that's a humbling experience. So, not to be proud, or cultivating humility, is something you can learn by walking. You humble yourself to nature around you, to the people that you meet on the road. Walking's a very humbling experience, and it allows you to see things in a new way. Expressing humility opens doors for understanding. Pride is the thing that really creates walls and doesn't allow you to see things in proper perspective. I think the best of me came out on that road, and I think more people should walk it."

Most people travel for personal reasons, and any lessons they take from it are personal as well. The dramas they play out along the highway are usually witnessed only by fellow travellers. Occasionally, however, one man's travel becomes so epic that those around him can't help but watch, admire and perhaps take inspiration. There have been journeys on the Trans-Canada Highway that have changed the entire nation and the world beyond.

Terry Fox was eighteen, a fine young athlete studying kinesiology, when he was diagnosed in 1977 with a rare form of cancer called osteogenic sarcoma. Immediately following the diagnosis, Terry's leg was amputated below the knee. His spirit, however, only strengthened. Using a prosthetic limb, Terry kept up his regime of long-distance running, telling his family that he was training for the Vancouver Marathon. But in the back of his mind was something much grander. As he was running, he was putting together a plan to run across the country to raise money for cancer research, figuring out how far he would go each day and where he would stop each night. Eventually, his plans were ready. He broke them first to his family.

Walking the length of the Trans-Canada, through rain, wind, buffeting traffic and isolating loneliness, eventually wore away Bhaktimarga Swami's pride. What emerged instead, he says, was openness and compassion.[74]

Darrell Fox, who ran with his brother Terry in the original Marathon of Hope, realized that his job on the run would be to make his brother laugh.[75]

"Was I surprised? Not for a minute," recalls his brother, Darrell, four years Terry's junior. "At that point Terry had run thousands of kilometres training for the Vancouver Marathon. To run a marathon you need to run a lot, but not the kind of miles Terry was putting in. I knew if Terry said he was going to do something, he did it—and to the best of his ability. I knew right away that he could do it. If he had told me he was going to run around the world twice I would have believed him."

And so, on April 12, 1980, Terry Fox began the Marathon of Hope, a one-man cross-Canada run along the Trans-Canada Highway to raise money for cancer research. He logged roughly 42 kilometres (26 miles) every day, rain or shine. The photographs of Terry running along the shoulder of the highway, followed by support vehicles, police escorts with flashing lights, and sometimes hundreds of people running along with him, have become iconic Canadian images of courage.

Darrell, who was only seventeen at the time, didn't think too much of it when he was asked to join Terry on the run. It would be a good way to miss a little school and graduate early, he thought. But on the first day of the run, he realized something much more powerful than that was about to happen. "The tears of joy, the dropped jaws—I knew right away I was witnessing history in the making," he says. Faced with the impact his brother's self-sacrifice was having on people lining the road, Darrell realized that he needed to make a contribution of his own.

"When I was asked to join up with Terry I had to take into consideration how I could be helpful," he says. "After realizing that I didn't have many skills, I knew that I had one thing that I was capable of doing and that was to make Terry laugh. And through what he was accomplishing— running, dealing with the media, making presentations—he needed to be

Fair weather or foul, Terry Fox logged 42 kilometres (26 miles) a day during his original run to raise money for cancer research. His tragic journey inspired a nation, then the entire world, to follow in his footsteps with annual Terry Fox runs.[76]

able to enjoy himself. So I was a practical joker. I think that there was probably not a town we went through that we didn't have a food fight."

Terry was to celebrate his 21st birthday in Gravenhurst, Ontario. Darrell, with other members of the Marathon of Hope entourage, plotted another practical joke. He would present his brother with an elaborate cake and then throw it in his face. "I was looking forward to it. Who wouldn't? Any younger sibling would love the opportunity to throw a cake in his brother's face. But that morning it was decided that Terry was having a bad day and perhaps I should just present the cake to him. Which I did. And Terry immediately took the cake and threw it in my face. They turned the tables on me. But it was an opportunity for us to relax and have a good time and Terry needed that."

Darrell often ran with Terry, always just slightly behind him, for Terry was intensely competitive and didn't like anyone in front. Terry was obsessed with mileage. Darrell says he demanded to know, to the foot, how far he'd run each day. And no wonder. Terry's marathon didn't just stick to the Trans-Canada but snaked through as many communities as possible in order to build support. By the time he was forced to quit, Terry had run 5,373 kilometres (3,339 miles). That was well over three-quarters of the distance back to Terry's home in Port Coquitlam, British Columbia, but with all the detours the marathon had made it to just outside of Thunder Bay.

The signs that Terry wasn't going to be able to complete the run were there, says Darrell. For two weeks before nearing Thunder Bay, he watched his brother grow uncharacteristically irritable and keep more and more to himself. And then, on September 1, when Darrell drove a support van up to the front of the procession for what he thought was a routine water break, Terry wasn't there. A police officer told Darrell that Terry had asked to go to the hospital.

"Right away, I knew there was something seriously wrong with him," says Darrell, whose voice still tightens at the memory. "By the time I found Terry, it had already been confirmed that the cancer that had taken his leg three years earlier had spread and was now in his lungs. But rather than Darrell Fox comforting Terry and telling his brother everything would be fine, it was just the opposite. It was Terry who was the strong one. One of the first things he said was that this was just going to give more meaning to what he'd accomplished, that this was happening for a reason."

Today, that reason can perhaps be found in the thousands of people who participate in Terry Fox Runs around the world. Before he died in 1981, Terry Fox had raised $24 million for cancer research. Over twenty years later, Terry Fox Runs raise that much again every single year.

Darrell is now national director of the Terry Fox Foundation. His narrow, lined faced and furrowed brow hint at the weight of being the kid brother of a legend.

"For the longest time after Terry passed away I made the mistake of trying to forget him, to try and reduce the impact he had on my life. That was just a way of dealing with it. It just wasn't the way it was supposed to end. Even up to the last day when Terry died, I thought he would bounce back and get on the road again and finish the Marathon of Hope. What Terry accomplished was a miracle. To run 42 kilometres (26 miles) every day on an artificial leg . . . I shake my head. I don't know how he did it.

"I live and breathe Terry Fox," Darrell says. "I'm immersed in the story. I can't get enough of it. This incredible opportunity to be in this role and to be Terry Fox's brother is something that I cherish every day."

A statue of Terry Fox now stands alongside the Trans-Canada Highway on which he logged so many kilometres, right at the point where the original Marathon of Hope ended. Although he never fulfilled his original goal of running across the entire country, his brave attempt cemented the role that the Trans-Canada plays in the national imagination: this highway is about more than getting from A to B. It's a road to measure yourself against, a road big enough to live on, a road on which you can make a point, either to yourself or to the whole world.

Faced with the task of building a single nation out of enough land for an entire continent, Canadians have become a people who travel enthusiastically, happily hopping into their cars with no more excuse than to see some new country and fill in a blank spot on the mental map of their nation. It took nearly a century before the longest road was finally built. But when it was, Canadians finally had a road worthy of them.

"Sure, I like driving," says Dennis Culver. "I like going from A to B and meeting the challenge of getting there. It gives me a mind's-eye picture of Canada. Not in enormous detail about every single section of it, but I have a view of it right now as I'm talking. I can see B.C. and imagine winding up through the twisty, torturous roads and climbing up the river valleys and going through to the mountains. And the flatness of the prairies, where you can see for tens of kilometres, where you can see the hazy lights of Regina getting brighter and brighter hour after hour. Then, all of a sudden, it's in your rear-view mirror. Driving past all the little pothole lakes and wooded areas of Ontario and then along the shores of Lake Superior and into Quebec, the St. Lawrence first of all, and then the Maritimes. The regions all have a different feel to them, and I feel I have a grasp of those differences."

The Culvers got home from their Trans-Canada odyssey in early September. For two days—two whole days—they stayed at home and did-

n't travel anywhere. Then they got restless. They all felt like going somewhere—maybe out to Long Beach on Vancouver Island. So Eleanor packed up the suitcases, Dennis fuelled up the bus, everyone piled in and off they drove.

Nothing beats a good road trip on a sunny day, and the Trans-Canada Highway, pictured here in Quebec's Gaspe region, offers some of the best cruising anywhere.[77]

IT BEGAN WITH THE RIVERS; NOW IT'S THE ROAD.

Today, Randy Bachman is a Canadian rock 'n' roll legend, but in the early 1960s, the Guess Who and Bachman–Turner Overdrive were still in the future. At 20 Bachman was just starting out, a guitarist with Chad Allan and the Expressions. He was still trying to develop his own style when music from a California band called The Beach Boys began to hit the radio in his Winnipeg hometown. It was an intriguing sound, but the words were puzzling to a prairie boy.

"I was in Winnipeg," he recalls. "It was wintertime when they first started playing 'Surfin' USA' on the radio. I didn't know what surfing was. You get on a board and you paddle out and you get on a wave. . . . How do you *get on* a wave?

"But when The Beach Boys came out with 'Little Deuce Coupe,' we all knew about getting on the road. Everybody knows about driving. I don't care what kind of music you're in, songs keep coming up about rollin' on down the highway." Bachman, who's spent more time than most on the road during a lifetime on tour buses travelling from gig to gig, was later to write some of them himself. BTO's hit "Let It Roll" may not have been inspired directly by the Trans-Canada, but it springs from the kind of experiences Bachman had on it.

"It's a parallel to keeping moving on in life," he says, his words spilling out as he warms to his subject. "The bad happens, the good happens, you keep driving on, you head into the horizon and you make the best of it. [Travelling's] always in your blood, and when it comes time to write songs, those themes just come out. For so many people, it's such a part of life that you end up writing about it."

For Canadians, perhaps, more than most. Of the more than 76 million overnight trips Canadians make every year, 93 percent are by road. And Canadians have more of it—and more of it to themselves—than almost any other people on earth. Canada has nearly 32 kilometres (20 miles) of road per 1,000 citizens. The United States has less than 24 (15 miles). France has a little more than 12 (eight miles), and Japan has only 8.5 (5.3 miles).

The open road, seen here near Moose Jaw, Saskatchewan, is a fact of Canadian life. And with more road per capita than almost any other nation, it's also one of its defining features.[79]

You can't write songs and ignore the road, says rock 'n' roll legend Randy Bachman. The image and experience of rolling down the highway can be used to say a lot about life.[78]

Cars to put on the road? We got 'em. At the turn of the millennium, there were 17.5 million registered vehicles in Canada, twelve times more than at the end of the Second World War and a little more than one vehicle for every two Canadians. And every year, dealers sell another 1.5 million new ones, give or take.

Canadians, of course, are forced by their geography into being a nation on wheels. Given the size of the place, you simply have to put some serious time in the driver's seat if you plan to get anywhere. But there's more than just necessity fuelling all that highway time. Canadians simply love to get out and move around. In 2002 Statistics Canada reported that we drove our cars more than 80 billion kilometres (50 billion miles) in the summer months alone. Over the course of a year, that works out to more than 9,650 kilometres (6,000 miles) for every Canadian man, woman and child. "That's

The Longest Road

what Canadians do," says John Ralston Saul. "They really like getting into their cars. Canadians actually love getting into some form of locomotion and moving across the country. The number of people I talk to every week who, at some point in a half-hour conversation, will talk to you about getting in the car and driving to some other part of Canada is amazing."

Canadians not only love to drive, they love to talk about it, says writer John Ralston Saul.[80]

Canada has plenty of justly renowned road cruises on which to indulge a passion for driving, from Alberta's Icefields Parkway to Nova Scotia's Cabot Trail, but the Trans-Canada Highway remains the granddaddy of all Canadian road trips. Its sheer length—nearly one-fifth of the earth's circumference and greater than that of the Great Wall of China—gives travel on the Trans-Canada an epic quality. A road of truly heroic proportions, it gives drivers a chance to live their own Odysseys. The distances are continental in scope. In Europe a five-hour drive can take you through three countries and as many cultures; in Canada, it gets you from Edmonton to Saskatoon. The landscapes are gargantuan. Driving through Europe, scenery changes from field to factory to town every fifteen minutes; driving through the Canadian Shield in northern Ontario means two days of lakes and trees and rocks. And the variety of scenery beside the longest road is just as outsized as its magnitude. The Trans-Canada offers two contrasting ocean coasts: the fog-shrouded rainforests of the Pacific and the rawboned North Atlantic. In between, mountain peaks roll into the distance like waves on wind-whipped water. There's the subtle play of gold, green and open blue on the prairies, great, dark forests, and lakes that would be called seas in any other country. All of it changes with the seasons. Few can say they know the whole of it, at all times. The longest road is long enough for a lifetime of journeys.

Most travellers, however, have a less grandiose experience of the Trans-Canada. Few tackle its full length or approach it as mountain to climb; mostly, it's an everyday route plied by truckers making a living and everyday drivers who choose the Trans-Canada for the bread-and-butter reason that it's the quickest—and often the only—way to get from A to B. It's this workaday side to the Trans-Canada that earns it the inevitable nickname "Canada's Main Street." There's some truth to that nickname, but it should also be approached with caution.

If this really were our showcase thoroughfare, Canada would be a poor sort of village. For most of its length, the Trans-Canada is only two lanes wide. Significant sections are twisty and slow, with speed limits under 100 kilometres an hour. In places it is pocked by potholes and marred by cracked asphalt. In the summer, traffic chokes it. In the winter, snow and ice sometimes shut sections of it down entirely. In many places, bad weather can make it downright dangerous. The Trans-Canada can't compare to the wide, smooth and remorselessly efficient interstates of the United States. The German autobahns, where every three minutes another black Mercedes is bearing down on you at 160 kilometres (100 miles) an hour, leave it far behind. Foreign travellers often express surprise at the poky nature of our vaunted national highway. Even in Canada, newer routes like the Coquihalla Highway in British Columbia make the Trans-Canada seem old and rambling.

And if main street is where most of the business gets done, the Trans-Canada has plenty of competition. True, nearly one-third of its traffic is commercial trucking. But east–west trade is declining in relative importance in the Canadian economy. Interprovincial trade, which mostly flows along routes such as the Trans-Canada, accounted for 27 percent of gross domestic product in 1981; by 1997 that had shrunk to 20 percent. More and more Canadian trade flows north–south.

If, however, main street is where people congregate, the place they go because it's where everyone is, then there is a sense in which that old tourist-brochure nickname suits. First of all, the Trans-Canada Highway is where we live. Something like 90 percent of Canadians live within a short drive of it. Secondly, if you drive at all in Canada, sooner or later you're going to leave some rubber on the Trans-Canada. Other countries, smaller or more densely populated, offer any number of ways to get around. Here, if you want to travel east or west for any distance, you're eventually going to steer to the nearest Trans-Canada on-ramp simply from necessity.

That means that over the years, the Trans-Canada has become a common source of image and memory for all Canadians. When Canadians call up a mental picture of their country, from the path through the mighty Selkirks of the Rogers Pass to the blue expanse of Lake Superior's Georgian Bay, they are likely recalling a scene witnessed through the window of a car travelling the Trans-Canada. The man-made landmarks, such as Sudbury's giant nickel or Wawa's goose, are part of that, too—kitschy, yes, but without them the road would be a lot less fun.

For the historically minded, the Trans-Canada is also replete with echoes of our common past. Drive the leg up British Columbia's Fraser Valley and you're joining the ghosts of gold-rush prospectors heading for the richly laden creeks of the Cariboo. Head west past Ontario's Lake of the Woods into the prairies and you're not far from where Canadian soldiers cut the old Dawson Road on their way to crush the Red River Rebellion. Through the prairies, where the highway is often within sight of the CPR, travellers can imagine the ringing steel and shouting navvies as they built the railway that first tied the country together. And the Yellowhead Highway, the Trans-Canada's northern branch between Portage la Prairie, Manitoba, and Edmonton, Alberta, echoes the old Carlton Trail, cut by Metis buffalo hunters driving Red River carts.

Most Canadians have some version of these visual and historic icons rattling around in the backs of their heads. From these icons come a shared knowledge of sights and sounds, the way the sunset looks, the way the air smells, how the people talk, the colour of the dirt and the rocks. This common understanding, derived from those inevitable trips down the Trans-Canada, becomes one of the building blocks of our sense of ourselves as a nation.

Like this 1960s couple enjoying a stop at a tourist camp along the Trans-Canada, the highway becomes associated with some of our strongest memories of fun and adventure.[81]

There is, however, more to a sense of home than an array of postcard memories. What we see and hear must also make us feel. And travelling the Trans-Canada, we can also learn to connect the landscape passing by the window with our hearts.

Because it's often the only choice for getting back and forth in this country, the Trans-Canada Highway inevitably becomes tied up with some of our most powerful memories. The Trans-Canada becomes the road to family weddings and summer holidays. Kids leave home on it, heading off to universities or jobs. A Trans-Canada trip becomes the prelude to a new career or a new life. Stories begin with "Remember that time we drove to . . ." The sights and experiences along the Trans-Canada become bound up in the major events of our lives, and the relationship between road and driver becomes one of intimate old friends. Like no other road in the nation, the Trans-Canada becomes a place of memory, where new journeys remind us of old ones, but no two are ever the same.

In 1972 Mark Giberson was a seventeen-year-old American living in Maine on the threshold of a big decision, maybe the biggest of his life. He disagreed with his country's war in Vietnam strongly enough to cross the border into Canada to avoid fighting in it. His father was disappointed and angry, but nevertheless agreed to drive Mark to New Brunswick, where the Gibersons had some roots. The two were driving down the Trans-Canada when Mark looked across and realized that tears were streaming down his 57-year-old father's face. They had just passed the road sign for the community of Tobik. His father explained, "I haven't heard that word or seen that word since I was a boy. Dad used to come over here fishing with his cousins in the summer." The mere name of the town had triggered a stream of memories about the Gibersons' Canadian past and

At seventeen, Mark Giberson made the life-changing decision to come to Canada to avoid fighting in the Vietnam War. He thought he was taking the Trans-Canada into a strange land, but his father's revelation on the trip north told him that he was bringing the family home.[82]

Now a Canadian citizen, Mark Giberson feels as much at home with the landscape along the Trans-Canada as did his Loyalist ancestors.[83]

The longest road.[84]

Canadian ancestors, stories Mark had never heard before. And on that road, driving through land their ancestors had settled and where many lay buried, Mark and his father reconciled. "You know, Mark, you've done the right thing," his father told him. "You've brought the family home."

Mark was returning to a place he'd never been. "This was the road that brought me home, but I didn't see it at the time," he says. "I thought it was a road taking me into the unknown."

That paradox of the unknown homeland is the secret to the longest road. Like the nation that built it, it's almost too big to really know. For the great majority of us, there will always be places on the Trans-Canada we've never been—Spuzzum, Gambo, Swift Current, St.-Jean-Port-Joli. There will always be new sights along its vast length and new people to meet. It will always remain a place of exploration, a place where the spirit of Alexander Mackenzie still lives. And at the same time, it's a familiar place, a place we understand and in which we recognize ourselves. It's Odyssey and Main Street, front porch and frontier, all at the same time.

Gavin Lumsden, the high-speed hitchhiker, may have said it best: "Wherever you see that No. 1 stuck in the middle of a maple leaf, you're home."

Photo Credits

Contents image courtesy Bruno Engler

Prologue image courtesy 180

Chapter 1 image courtesy the Culver family

1 Image courtesy the Culver family

2 Image courtesy theNational Archives of Canada PA68217

3 Image courtesy the Archives of Ontario 10005701

4 Image courtesy the Saskatchewan Archives Board 61-269-21

5 Image courtesy the Saskatchewan Archives Board S-B 12686

6 Image courtesy the National Archives of Canada PA126333

7 Image courtesy the Culver family

Chapter 2 image courtesy Virginia Hemingson

8 Image courtesy Henry Youle Hind, the National Archives of Canada NMC-7051

9 Image courtesy National Archives of Canada

10 Image courtesy the National Archives of Canada C21915

11 Image courtesy Burt Brown

12 Image courtesy Lorne Findley

13 Image courtesy Lorne Findley

14 Image courtesy National Archives of Canada

15 Image courtesy the National Archives of Canada PA19347

16 Image courtesy Burt Brown

17 Image courtesy Burt Brown

18 Image courtesy Burt Brown

19 Image courtesy the National Archives of Canada PA196490

20 Image courtesy Bruno Engler

21 Image courtesy the National Archives of Canada PA210245

Chapter 3 image courtesy Andrew and Gavin Lumsden

22 Image courtesy the Culver family

23 Image courtesy Barbra Mitchell

24 Image courtesy Andrew and Gavin Lumsden

25 Image courtesy Bonita Garrett

26 Image courtesy Bonita Garrett

27 Image courtesy Danya Gabruch

28 Image courtesy Danya Gabruch

29 Image courtesy Danya Gabruch

30 Image courtesy Danya Gabruch

31 Image courtesy Alan and Donna Kelly

32 Image courtesy Alan and Donna Kelly

33 Image courtesy Danya Gabruch

34 Image courtesy Danya Gabruch

Chapter 4 image courtesy Bruno Engler

35 Image courtesy Danya Gabruch

36 Image courtesy the Saskatchewan Archives Board 54-161-05

37 Image courtesy the Saskatchewan Archives Board 57-274-142

38 Image courtesy Bruno Engler

39 Image courtesy Banff National Park

40 Image courtesy the National Archives of Canada PA800449

41 Image courtesy Bruno Engler

42 Image courtesy Bruno Engler

Chapter 5 image courtesy Banff National Park

43 Image courtesy the National Archives of Canada PA191984

44 Image courtesy Tony Dias

45 Image courtesy the National Archives of Canada PA111479

46 Image courtesy Danya Gabruch

47 Image courtesy the Archives of Ontario 10006376

48 Image courtesy the Melville-Ness Collection, Saskatchewan Archives
    Board S-MN-13 2590

49 Image courtesy Danya Gabruch

50 Image courtesy Danya Gabruch

51 Image courtesy the National Archives of Canada PA151721

52 Image courtesy Danya Gabruch

Chapter 6 image courtesy the Culver family

53 Image courtesy the Culver family

54 Image courtesy the Walkem family

55 Image courtesy the Walkem family

56 Image courtesy Danya Gabruch

57 Image courtesy Dennis Edwards

58 Image courtesy Dennis and Allie Edwards

59 Image courtesy Danya Gabruch

60 Image courtesy Shelly Gwilliam

61 Image courtesy June Wagman, Summerberry School

62 Image courtesy June Wagman

63 Image courtesy Lillian Williams

64 Image courtesy Danya Gabruch

65 Image courtesy Lillian Williams

66 Image courtesy Danya Gabruch

67 Image courtesy Danya Gabruch

68 Image courtesy Danya Gabruch

69 Image courtesy Danya Gabruch

Chapter 7 image courtesy Gail Harvey, photographer, the Terry Fox Foundation

70 Image courtesy Alan and Donna Kelly

71 Image courtesy Danya Gabruch

72 Image courtesy Danya Gabruch

73 Image courtesy Danya Gabruch

74 Image courtesy Danya Gabruch

75 Image courtesy Danya Gabruch

76 Image courtesy Gail Harvey, photographer, the Terry Fox Foundation

77 Image courtesy the National Archives of Canada PA211688

Epilogue image courtesy Bruno Engler

78 Image courtesy Danya Gabruch

79 Image courtesy the Saskatchewan Archives Board 60-482-01

80 Image courtesy Danya Gabruch

81 Image courtesy the National Archives of Canada PA211689

82 Image courtesy Mark Giberson

83 Image courtesy Danya Gabruch

84 Image courtesy the Archives of Ontario 10006375

Bob Weber grew up just a few blocks from the Trans-Canada Highway in Swift Current, Sask., and over the years he's driven across most of it. Originally trained as a musician, he slowly drifted into writing and currently works in Edmonton as a reporter for the Canadian Press wire service, for whom he's written about everything from mad cows to angry politicians. Weber also covers northern Canada for CP and has travelled the Arctic from Pangnirtung to Tuktoyaktuk. Weber's three previous books, including an anecdotal history of Saskatchewan and a ghost-written autobiography of hockey legend Bill Hunter, betray a strong love for the stories of Western Canada. Weber also worked with noted horseman Chris Irwin on a book about horses and personal growth which has been reprinted worldwide.